DOWSING

Ancient origins and modern uses

by

Rodney Davies

The Aquarian Press
An Imprint of HarperCollins*Publishers*

The Aquarian Press
An Imprint of GraftonBooks
A Division of HarperCollins*Publishers*
77–85 Fulham Palace Road
Hammersmith, London W6 8JB

Published by The Aquarian Press 1991
1 3 5 7 9 10 8 6 4 2

© Rodney Davies 1991

Rodney Davies asserts the moral right to
be identified as the author of this work

All the drawings, with the exception
of Figures 1, 15, 16 and 17, are
by the author

A CIP catalogue record for this book
is available from the British Library

ISBN 1 85538 073 0

Typeset by G&M, Raunds, Northamptonshire
Printed in Great Britain by
HarperCollinsManufacturing, Glasgow

CONTENTS

I would like to thank those people who took the time and trouble to talk to me about their experience of dowsing. Without their contribution this book would have been a meagre work. My thanks also go to Bill Mundl and Dr Judith Whitehead, both of Concordia University, Montreal, and to Dr F.W. Flitney of St Andrew's University, Scotland. This book is dedicated, with respect and affection, to them all.

INTRODUCTION

Dowsing in its traditional guise is the art of finding substances or objects hidden in the ground, like water, oil, minerals, pipes and cables, archaeological relics, and so on, by means of a forked stick or some other type of divining rod, or a pendulum. Yet it can also be used to detect the whereabouts of lost objects and persons, or the site of disease in a living body. Thus it can be defined as the practice of finding things, whether above or below ground, whose location is not known. The person who holds the divining rod or pendulum is called a dowser, although owing to the frequent use of these aids to find water, he or she is commonly referred to as a 'water-diviner' or 'water-witch'.

The names 'water-diviner' and 'water-witch' quite naturally suggest that dowsing is a magical, and therefore superstitious, practice, one engaged in by unsophisticated rustics who know no better. Scientists in general take this view, although there are a few brave souls, like Dr Bernard Grad of Montreal, who have investigated dowsing and discovered that it cannot be dismissed so lightly. For dowsers often find what they are looking for, when previous attempts by geologists, hydrologists and other scientific professionals have ended in failure.

It is perhaps the very success of dowsers to pin-point their target that sticks in the craw of scientists. How can anyone, they ask, armed with nothing more than a forked stick, locate substances often buried hundreds of feet down in the ground, when the most modern and sophisticated instruments and techniques cannot do so? And they argue that if a dowser is successful, he or she is either 'lucky' or has a shrewd eye for local landscape features, which suggest, consciously or unconsciously, where the substance is to be found. In this way they dismiss dowsing as a haphazard, if not fraudulent activity, unworthy of notice, whose practitioners fool nobody but themselves.

And no dowser is right every time, but then neither is a doctor when diagnosing a disease, a geologist looking for oil, or a hydrologist searching for water. Like them, dowsers have their 'off' days and their misses. Yet the fact that they are often called in after the 'experts' have failed, suggests that their art is worthy of trial, if only as a last resort.

But while scientists remain highly sceptical about the validity of dowsing, there is a generally sympathetic attitude towards it among the public at large, who instinctively feel that science does not have all the answers.

It is for this reason that I have written this book. It is designed to give you, the reader, an outline and a history of the subject, along with instructions as to how you, too, can dowse. Indeed, the exciting thing about dowsing is that most people can do it, if they would but try. In other words, you don't need to possess some special talent to dowse.

And take my word for it, few things in life are more remarkable or thrilling than the first time that one's dowsing rod turns downwards, seemingly pulled by some unknown force towards the ground. It will be the moment when you realize, as Shakespeare so ably puts it, that 'there are more things in heaven and earth, Horatio, than are dreamt of in your philosophy'.

Good dowsing!

In autumn life he stood within the grounds
Where joyous voices seldom can be heard.
But from the distance shouts from village green
Were carried, mingling soft with nearer notes.
A fresh'ning breeze, with just a hint of rain,
Was slanting all the branches round about
The sheltered garden in which thrushes sang;
And lengthening twilight merging into night
Brought memories of happier boyhood days.
And near at hand were clust'ring hazel boughs,
From which the catkins, ripe and golden-green,
Swung loosely in the misty evening breeze.
Lightly he touched them with a calloused hand,
And in his palm was poured a dust of gold.

From *The Dowser* by Herbert Cole

CHAPTER ONE

THE WOOD SPIRITS

For know by lot from *Jove* I am the power
Of this fair wood, and live in oak'n bower,
To nurse the saplings tall, and curl the grove
With ringlets quaint, and wanton windings wove.
And all my plants I save from nightly ill,
Of noisome winds, and blasting vapours chill.
And from the boughs brush off the evil dew,
And heal the harms of thwarting thunder blew,
Or what the cross dire-looking planet smites,
Or hurtfull worm with canker'd venom bites.

From *Arcades* by John Milton

The Origins of Dowsing

Dowsing was unknown in the ancient world, and indeed it seems to be a comparatively recently-discovered technique, the first unequivocal reference to it appearing in Sebastian Munster's *Cosmographia Universalis*, which was published in Germany in 1500. Munster calls the rod used a *virgula divina*, or divining rod (see Figure 1), while his fellow-countryman Agricola, writing about mining operations in his *De re metallica*, published in 1540, refers to it as a *virgula furcata*, or forked rod. These texts suggest that dowsing originated in Germany, probably among miners of Saxony and the Hartz mountains, sometime in the fifteenth century.

Figure 1: Early sixteenth-century dowsers at work.

The Magical Properties of Trees and Woods

But if dowsing was unknown to the ancients, the beliefs that they held certainly contributed to its later discovery. For it was their notions about the divinity of trees and the magical properties of wood, coupled with their belief in underworld deities, that persisted long after the fall of Rome and which ultimately led to the dowsing of subterranean metal ores.

Pre-Christian Europe was a realm of trees. Vast forests covered most of the landscape, making travel both difficult and dangerous. Towns and villages were sited by the sides of rivers and on the banks of lakes, where the vegetation was thinner and easier to remove, and where there was a ready supply of water, or alternatively on the tops of hills. But the trees were ever-present, providing wood for building, nuts and fruits for eating, and game. Beneath their constantly rustling leaves and branches lived all manner of dangerous animals, like wolves, bears and boars, as well as, or so it was believed, a variety of spiritual beings, most of them potentially harmful. In fact the forests were frightening places in which people could easily become lost and die.

The awe in which the forests were held by the people who lived on their fringes derived largely from the latter's animistic beliefs. They thought that everything in nature was alive, not simply the animals with which they shared the forests and the trees which formed them, but the very rocks beneath their feet, the metals with which they fashioned their weapons and tools, and the water that they drank.

These inert substances were alive because they were all homes to a spirit, as were animate creatures. Each tree housed a spirit, and it was a rash man who dared lop off a branch or cut one down without taking the necessary propitiatory precautions beforehand. Indeed, no one who has heard the screaming noise that a tree makes when it is felled can deny that it sounds like a death cry, nor that if such an act released an angry spirit, some form of violent retribution must be expected. This is why wood in these early times was probably taken from trees which had fallen of their own accord.

The Ancient Divinities

Yet just as in nature some phenomena or objects are more spectacular and threatening than others, so it was believed that some spirits were more powerful than the rest. Those spirits inhabiting the sun, the moon, the sky, the air, and the earth itself, were held to be greater than their fellows, as were those of the sea to the people who lived by its shore. A violent thunderstorm is a frightening event, and the being who caused it was more to be feared than one inhabiting a quiet pond. Such spirits became elevated into gods and goddesses, who had authority over the lesser deities, and of course over the world of man.

These numerous divinities were held to be jealous and unpredictable. They could on the one hand dispense blessings in the form of good health, a successful hunt, or a bounteous harvest, but they could just as easily cause disease, blight the crops, and ensure defeat in battle. It therefore became imperative to know how to propitiate or favourably influence them, a function that was assigned to a specialist, the tribal wise-man or shaman, who possessed a greater knowledge of the spirit world than did the ordinary person and who knew the correct rituals and magical practices to bring good fortune to his people. For while praying directly to the gods might bring results, it was far more likely to be successful when accompanied by sacrifice and ceremony, which encouraged the deity concerned to grant one's wishes. Magic was also carried on in daily life. Not only did everyone wear amulets and magic stones for protection, but even ordinary activities like baking, lighting a fire, and herding the livestock, were regulated by all manner of 'dos and don'ts', whose aim was to encourage the spirits to be helpful and to look favourably upon those concerned.

The Scandinavian Creation Myths

In northern Europe it was believed that mankind had actually sprung from trees. One myth recounts how the three gods Odin, Hoenir and Lodur were travelling through the landscape of the newly formed earth, which had been created from the bodily parts of the giant Ymir, when they encountered two large dead trees. These they decided to make into human beings, transforming one into a man, the other into a woman. That done, Odin gave them breath, Hoenir gave them a soul and intelligence, and Lodur gave them bodily warmth and the rosy colour of life, so making them living people. The man was called Ask (meaning 'Ash') and the woman Embla (or 'Vine'), and it is from this pair, according to the Scandinavians, that all mankind is descended. Ask and Embla are the exact counterparts of the Biblical Adam and Eve, although in the Hebrew myth Adam was formed 'of the dust of the ground', and Eve, at a later date, was fashioned from one of Adam's ribs.

These different accounts of the origins of the first human pair probably reflect the different landscapes inhabited by the myth makers: the Scandinavians lived in a world of trees, the

Jews in one of dusty deserts, where trees were a comparative rarity.

The Myth of Yggdrasill — The World Tree

Furthermore, the Scandinavians also thought that while the world had been formed from the body of the giant Ymir, it had at its centre a huge tree called Yggdrasill. This World Tree spread its branches out over both the heavens and the earth, and sent three massive roots down into the ground. One of the roots grew into Asgard, the home of the gods, and beneath it was found the Well of Urd, the sacred spring of fate. Another root entered the kingdom of the frost-giants, and below it was the spring of Mimir, whose clear water was infused with wisdom and understanding. The third root entered Niflhel, the underworld, and under it was the fountain Huergelmir, from which the rivers of the earth sprang. It was said that Odin happily gave up the sight of one of his eyes to be allowed to drink from the spring of Mimir, thereby acquiring divine wisdom. And just as one of the roots of the World Tree grew above the spring of fate, so too was the destiny of each person written upon its leaves. The tree itself was always in leaf, thereby symbolizing the continuance of the human race, but when one leaf fell it brought about the death of the individual whose name was written on it.

The myth of Yggdrasill, the World Tree, emphasizes the connection between trees and water, which perhaps explains why tree boughs are traditionally used to find water, and shows how trees became the source of man's greatest gift, wisdom, and why they were so often consulted about the future.

Odin

The god Odin is more familiarly known to us as Woden, whose name survives as Wednesday — Woden's day. This suggests that the most propitious day of the week on which to dowse is Wednesday. The Romans identified Odin (or Woden), the northern god of war, intelligence, wisdom and poetry, with their Mercury, whose name survives in the French *Mercredi*. And we speak of the northern god Tiw every time we say 'Tuesday' (Tiw's day), of Thor every time we say 'Thursday' (Thor's day), and of the goddess Frigg or Frija every time we say 'Friday' (Frigg's day). Hence the deities of our ancestors are still with us, and we should be glad that they are.

The Greek Creation Myths

The ancient Greeks also developed a complex mythology to account for the creation of the world and of mankind, and to describe and explain the nature and responsibilities of their various deities. They believed that the sky, the sea, and the underworld, were respectively under the control of the three divine brothers, Zeus, Poseidon, and Hades, and their spouses, while the earth, the home of man, was common to them all. Of the other major deities, Athene, Hermes, Aphrodite, Apollo, Artemis, Ares and Dionysus were said to be the children of Zeus who, as ruler of the sky, was the king of the gods, whereas Hephaestus, the god of fire and the forge, and Demeter, the corn goddess, were not. All of these divine beings, with the exception of Hades, lived on Mount Olympus, where also dwelt, to make up the holy twelve, Zeus's wife Hera.

The gods Hades and Hermes both have a direct relevance to dowsing and must therefore be considered in some detail.

Hades

Hades, as the ruler of the dead, was eternally separated from the other gods and found few worshippers among the Greeks. Indeed, he was feared rather than revered. Yet because he had control of everything in the earth, such as underground water, mineral ores, notably those from which tin and copper (the ingredients of bronze), iron, gold and silver are obtained, and gemstones, he was also more cheerfully called Pluto, which derives from the Greek word *plouton*, meaning 'riches'. In both these aspects he was regarded as The Wealthy One, as not only did his realm include the riches of the earth, but was always being added to by his henchman Death.

The Underworld

The Greeks pictured the underworld as a gloomy, mournful place, where the souls of the dead existed as insubstantial replicas of their physical selves, but lacking either intelligence or wit. However, as Homer tells us in the *Odyssey*, the dead could be imparted rationality by being allowed to drink blood, which is why Odysseus, on making the dangerous journey to the threshold of the underworld, was required to dig a pit and to allow the blood from the cut throats of a barren heifer and a black sheep to run into it. He did this in order to learn his future from the seer Teiresias, who duly performed this task on drinking the blood. Hence the dead, while conceived of as continuing to exist as twittering shades, retained the same abilities as they had had in life, although these could only manifest through the medium of blood sacrifice.

The Use of the Magical Rod

The magical rod or staff is first encountered in connection with soothsaying. Let us take Teiresias as an example. He was the most celebrated Greek seer, blind like Homer, and being the contemporary in myth with Oedipus and Heracles, probably lived — if indeed he actually existed — during the thirteenth century BC. He was apparently not born with prophetic insight, but received it upon being blinded by either Athene or Hera, who also gave him, at the same time, a rod made of cornel-wood, a tree sacred to the god Cronus (or Saturn). And because the name Teiresias means 'he who delights in signs', it is possible that, not being able to see, he manipulated the rod in some way and foretold the future from its movements. The cornel (*Cornus sanquinea*), better known as dogwood, is a deciduous shrub found commonly in both Britain and Europe, whose Latin genus name *Cornus* means 'horny' and derives from the hard and horny nature of its wood.

Cronus, the father of Zeus, Poseidon and Hades, was said to possess an adamantine sickle, which he used to castrate and thus usurp his own father Uranus, and which identifies him as a lunar deity. He was, in fact, the god of the Old Moon. The Moon, as ruler of the night, has associative connections with the underworld, water, and the feminine qualities of intuition, inspiration, irrationality, and so on. In fact Teiresias was the second spectre to appear to Odysseus, the first being one of his former shipmates, Elpenor, which links him with lunar intuition, 2 being one of the two numbers associated with the Moon. And his ghost carries 'a gold rod in his hand'.

The use of a rod as an instrument of magic occurs in the story of Odysseus's encounter with the witch-goddess Circe, a daughter of the Sun, who lives on the island of Aeaea, in a house standing, as befits a deity, in a grove of trees. When the wily Odysseus and his men landed on the island, Odysseus, sensing danger, divided the party into two squads, took command of one, and then drew lots to determine which should make the first approach to Circe's magic grove. The winner was the party led by Eurylochus, who made their way to the witch's house where they were cordially received, invited inside (although Eurylochus, who was evidently as canny as Odysseus, remained without and observed what happened) and then fed a meal laced with a magic drug:

> Which eat, she toucht them with a rod that wrought
> Their transformations far past human wonts;
> Swine's snouts, swine's bodies took they, bristles, grunts,
> But still retain'd the souls they had before,
> Which made them mourn their bodies' change the more.[1]

And having changed the luckless sailors into pigs, the treacherous Circe drove them into pens and threw them 'oak-mast, and beech, and cornel-fruit' to eat.

This of course posed Odysseus with a problem. How could he resist the magic rod of Circe, obtain the information he needed from the goddess, and rescue his companions? The answer was supplied by the god Hermes who arrived on the scene and gave him the antidote to Circe's magic — a plant called Moly, which has a black root and a milk-white flower, and which may be, as Robert Graves suggests, the wild cyclamen. And indeed, thus protected, Odysseus achieved his ends.

Hermes

Hermes was the busiest of the Greek deities. We know him best as the messenger of the gods, but he was also the protector of strangers and travellers, gave luck in trade, commerce and gambling, governed invention, music, mathematics, and writing, promoted skill in speech, and looked after thieves and liars. He was also the god of magic and intelligence. But more importantly where we are concerned, he was the god who brought the death-like state of sleep, gave foreknowledge of the future, and conducted the dead to Hades' realm. In the latter role he was really a god of the dead, despite living as he did atop Mount Olympus. Homer tells us that he carried a gold rod, which in course of time became portrayed as a *caduceus*, a winged rod about which are entwined two serpents.

It is probable that the 'gold rod' carried by Hermes was not made of gold but of hazel-wood, for the hazel tree was held to be sacred to him. The hazel (*Corylus avellana*), although typically met with as a low-growing shrub, will develop into a tree of some 30 ft (10 m) in height if allowed to do so, and is made conspicuous in the spring by its golden-yellow catkins, which reach a length of about 2 in (50 mm) and are in themselves little 'gold rods'. If we remember that it was Hermes who regularly descended into Hades' subterranean realm, where are found the treasures of the earth, it is not surprising to discover that hazel is the tree from which dowsers traditionally cut their divining rods.

Trees and the Gods

Trees, as I have already mentioned, were an omnipresent feature of the ancient landscape, and this was due not only to their numbers but also to their size. Tall trees stretch their branches high into the sky, where Zeus and the other blessed gods resided, and sink their roots deep down into the ground, the realm of Hades. This necessarily gave the spirits that inhabited them, known as dryads to the Greeks, a special relationship with both. In fact trees were regarded so highly by the early Greeks and other ancient peoples, that each type of tree became linked with, and thus sacred to, one or other of the gods. We have already noted that the hazel was sacred to Hermes, and the cornel, along with the alder, to Cronus. Similarly, the oak was sacred to Zeus (the Roman Jupiter), the willow and the pomegranate to his wife Hera (or Juno), the cypress and the black poplar to Hades (or Father Dis), the ash to Poseidon (or Neptune), the olive to Athene (or Minerva), the apple to Aphrodite (or Venus), the holly to Ares (or Mars), the vine to Dionysus (or Bacchus), the palm to both Artemis (or Diana) and Apollo, although it is the laurel that is chiefly linked with the latter, and the birch to Helius, the sun-god.

These sacred associations of god and tree gave each tree a specific type of magical power, which derived both from the spirit that lived within it and also from the more powerful god or goddess to which it was sacred. This perhaps explains why forked sticks cut from trees other than hazel, such as the apple and the willow, are also used for dowsing. And in antiquity the trees themselves were often consulted for knowledge of the future. At Dodona, for example, the sounds made by the sacred oak's branches rustling together, or those made by the brazen vessels hung from them, clanking together, were interpreted by Zeus's priests, the Helli, as the god's own prophetic words. Homer tells us in the *Iliad* that the Helli 'leave their feet unwashed and sleep on the ground', which suggests a close connection between the earth and prophetic inspiration. He also informs us elsewhere that to pray to Hades, a suppliant must either strike the ground with his bare hands or with rods.

Divination using Wood Strips

More pertinent, in view of the fact that dowsing apparently originated in Germany, was the use of wood strips for divination by the ancient Germans. The Roman historian Tacitus (c.56–115 AD) records in his *Germanica*, that when a German family or tribe had to make an important decision, such as whether or not to make war, a branch was cut from a nut-bearing tree and sliced into strips. Certain signs were incised on each strip, which were then tossed on to a white cloth laid on the ground. A priest, after offering a prayer to the gods, next stepped forward and, looking skywards, picked up three of the strips, whose signs were interpreted. If their meaning was favourable, the enterprise went ahead; if not, it didn't. Nut-bearing trees include the beech, the hazel, the walnut, and the sweet-chestnut, all of which might have been used for such divination, and it cannot be a coincidence that one of them, the hazel, became the favoured tree of dowsers.

The Magic Rod in Roman Mythology

Another link between a rod and the subterranean world occurs in Virgil's *Aeneid*, which recounts how Aeneas, journeying from sacked Troy to found a new city in Italy, stopped at Cumae in Euboea to visit the prophetic Sibyl, who resided there in a cave which is one of the entrances to the underworld. Having been apprised of his fate by the Sibyl, he begged of her to be allowed to enter the nether regions to see his dead father once more. She told him:

> If you choose to give yourself up to this mad adventure, hear what tasks must first be accomplished. Hiding in a tree's thick shade there is a bough, and it is golden, with both leaves and pliant stems of gold. It is dedicated as sacred to Juno of the Lower World. All the forest gives it protection, and it is enclosed by shadows within a valley of little light. Yet permission for descending to earth's hidden world is never granted to any who has not first gathered this golden-haired produce from its tree, for beautiful Proserpine has directed that this must be brought to her as her especial offering. Each time the bough is torn from its place another never fails to appear, golden like the first, and its stem grows also leaves of gold. So therefore you must lift up your eyes and seek to discern this bough, find it as required of you, and pick it boldly. Then, if it is indeed you whom the Fates are calling, it will come willingly and easily; if not, by no strength will you master it, nor even hack it away with a hard blade of steel.[2]

Thus informed, Aeneas entered the vast forest of tall spruce, oak, ash and rowan trees, where two doves led him to the tree, a holm-oak, upon which grew the golden bough, and from which he 'snatched it down at once. It resisted, but avidly he broke it off, and carried it to the home of the prophetic Sibyl.'

The holm-oak (*Quercus ilex*) is not native to Britain, but has been introduced and grown in many of our parks. It is an evergreen, and is further distinguished by the dark colour of its bark, which is probably why it was associated with the underworld.

We thus find that in ancient literate societies there was a belief in the magical powers of trees, powers that were also present in the rods cut from them, and that such rods could not only be used to perform magical transformations but gave their owner access to the underworld. These beliefs were spread by Roman colonization (if they were not already held) to all parts of Western Europe and eventually became part of common folklore. Indeed, our fairy tales are full of stories of witches who perform magic by means of a wand, and our modern conjurors still wave a wand or rod to carry out theirs. And undoubtedly it was this folk belief that led to the use of rods for dowsing, although we cannot say who first used one in this way, nor for that matter exactly when.

CHAPTER TWO

DOWSING DEVICES

Nay Lady sit; if I but wave this wand,
Your nerves are all chain'd up in alabaster,
And you are a statue; or as Daphne was
Root-bound, that fled Apollo.

From *A Mask Presented at Ludlow Castle* by John Milton

The Y-Shaped Rod

The traditional dowsing or divining rod is a forked or Y-shaped branch cut from a hazel, apple, willow or birch tree, although boughs from other trees such as elm and maple are sometimes used. Indeed, in America the peach is the most popular tree from which to take a dowsing rod, the willow being the second favourite. The arms of the forked branch are usually cut to a length of about 18 ins (45 cm) while its stem, which serves as the pointer, can be cut as short as 2 ins or as long as 6 ins (15 cm). These measurements are by no means critical, however, and some dowsers prefer their rods to be either smaller or larger in size (see Figure 2).

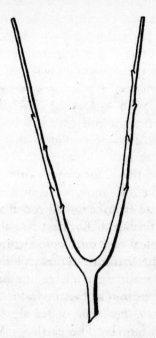

Figure 2: The traditional Y-shaped dowsing rod.

The basic dowsing rod is therefore easily obtained, and if you have an apple tree in your garden and a pair of secateurs, there is no reason why you can't supply yourself with one in a few moments. Should the branch you select bear small side branches, simply trim these off neatly. Many dowsers only use a green or freshly-cut rod, but this is perhaps because the rod needs to be supple as its arms are bent in the dowser's hands (dead and very dry wood would of course split or break when bent).

The Ancient Magic Rod

But why is a Y-shaped rod used when the ancient magic rod, which is the probable ancestor of the dowsing rod, was a simple straight rod? The answer to this question is complicated by the fact that it is quite possible to dowse with a straight rod, and indeed some dowsers still do. The forked rod apparently developed from a straight rod, as the earliest pictures of dowsers in operation show them using what appears to be a straight rod that has been partially split lengthwise, so as to provide two arms that could be held in the hands (see Figure 1).

This happened, I think, for two reasons. The first is due to the mechanics of the rod's movements: it is quite simply easier to obtain a response from a forked rod than a straight one. The second, and probably the most important, stems from the system of magical and astrological correspondences that were current in the fifteenth century. The world was then envisaged as being made up of a large number of opposites — opposite sexes, opposite qualities, opposite substances, etc — whose 'gender' was either male or female. Now dowsing, by its very nature, is female. The earth — Mother Earth — wherein are hidden those things that the dowser wishes to find, is female. Water itself is female, as is the wood from which the rod is made. The intuitive sense that a dowser may use is certainly female. A straight rod, however, having a phallic shape, is male and therefore is magically inappropriate or 'unlucky' for such a feminine activity. The forked rod, on the other hand, is decidedly female. Take a look at Figure 2 again, and think back to those diagrams of the female reproductive system that you saw in your school biology textbook. The two are almost identical. The two arms of the rod represent the two fallopian tubes, the point where they join the womb, and the stem the vagina. The wooden forked-rod is thus a quintessentially feminine tool, ideal for performing the quintessentially feminine task of searching for water and metal ores hidden in the dark womb of Mother Earth.

But none the less most dowsers agree that you can dowse with almost anything, which is why all manner of articles, such as pairs of scissors, clay pipes, pitchforks, lengths of baling twine, and walking sticks, have been substituted for the forked rod, along with the ever-popular pendulum. And a friend of mine, bookseller John George of Montreal, told me that his father regularly and successfully dowsed with a crowbar on his prairie farm.

L-Shaped Rods

However, the most widely-used alternative to the traditional forked rod are L-shaped rods that can be snipped from wire

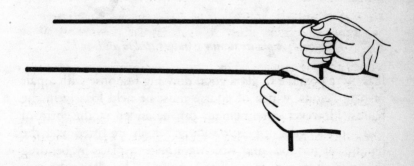

Figure 3: Dowsing with L-rods.

coat hangers. As wire coat hangers constantly proliferate in our wardrobes, it is nice to know that something useful can be made from them, while at the same time reducing their numbers! L-shaped or angle rods were first used by the American dowser Louis Matacia, who euphemistically calls them 'rudders', and who taught members of the U.S. Marine Corps how to find the underground tunnels dug by the Vietcong with them. Two L-rods are held parallel, one in each hand, and they indicate the site of the tunnel or whatever else is being searched for by moving together or by swinging outwards (see Figure 3).

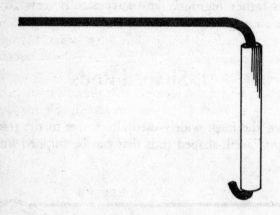

Figure 4: A plastic tubing handle fitted to an L-rod.

It is quite possible to get a good dowsing response with a pair of bare L-rods, which of course must be held loosely in the hands. However, a refinement can be added in the form of two short lengths of plastic tubing, which are fitted over the handles of the rods and which are held in place by bending the ends of the rods round (see Figure 4). This allows the rods to turn easily no matter how tightly the plastic tubing is gripped.

The Pendulum

The other basic piece of dowsing equipment is the pendulum, which can be easily made from a short length of cotton thread or fine string and a plumb-bob of some kind. Virtually anything can be used for the latter, as its function is only to weight the string, and wedding rings, coins with holes in them, and conkers have all been employed. (In fact children in Britain once successfully dowsed for lost objects with a cotton reel hung at the end of a piece of thread.) Wooden plumb-bobs are particularly popular, as are crystals, whose owners like to imagine possess some intrinsic mystical qualities that make dowsing with them easier. Manufactured pendulums can be purchased quite cheaply from most 'occult' shops, and come in a variety of shapes and sizes. If you make your own pendulum, remember that the cotton or string need only be about 7 ins (17.5 cm) in length. Figure 5 shows a number of pendulum types.

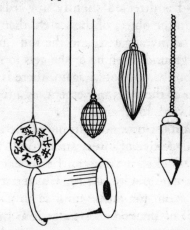

Figure 5: Different types of pendulums.

The Y-shaped dowsing rod and the L-shaped rods are primarily used for field dowsing, i.e. outdoor work, while the pendulum is mainly used for indoor work, notably for map dowsing. But there is no hard and fast rule about this; some dowsers use a Y-shaped rod for map dowsing, and some use a pendulum to field dowse. Hence the method employed depends upon the personal preference of the diviner, which is why you should experiment with all three devices in order to discover which suits you best.

The 'Pull' of the Rod

The Y-shaped dowsing rod is held as illustrated in Figure 6. Each hand — palms turned upwards — grips the end of one of the fork's arms with sufficient force to bend them outwards and thereby impart an incipient rotational impetus to the rod. The elbows are kept close to the sides of the body, and the stem of the rod is directed slightly upwards. The dowser, concentrating on the object of the search, then walks over the ground-site to be investigated, and the rod turns downwards to point at the ground when he or she gets to the place where the target lies buried. But once again, there is no uniformity in the direction of the rod's movement, as a few dowsers find that it turns upwards for them.

The downward (or upward) turning of the rod can be, and frequently is, suggestive of a very strong 'pull' on it. Amateur dowser Bob Weeks, manager of the Faculty Services Computer Centre at Concordia University, learned his dowsing skills from his father, and says, 'Dad remembers having the pull of the rod so strong from the tip, that the green apple wood would twist within the bark where he was holding it.'

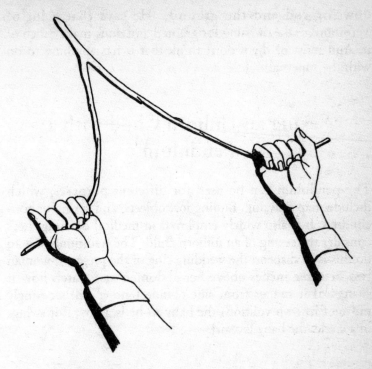

Figure 6: How the Y-shaped dowsing rod is held.

Bob, a lanky, deep-voiced Vermonter, whose ancestors came to New England from Old England in the seventeenth century, readily admits that he doesn't fully understand why the rod moves. 'It's always a question,' he told me, 'of whether one is being informed by the divining rod or has informed it of something. I've always gone out looking for water and not for other materials or missing objects, so my approach is to basically empty my mind. I'm not concentrating on finding water. And there's nothing particularly psychic about the feeling when you do find it. I don't have any other sensation than a sudden strong force acting between the tip of the dowsing rod and the ground.' He says that a lot of Vermonters take dowsing for granted and don't make much of it. And most of them don't think that it has anything to do with the supernatural.

Sexing an Unborn Child with a Pendulum

The pendulum can be used for different purposes, which include map dowsing, finding lost objects, and sexing unborn children. It is also widely employed in medical dowsing. Let's consider the sexing of an unborn child. The traditional way to do this is to suspend the wedding ring of the pregnant woman two or three inches above her abdomen and watch how it swings. If it swings from side-to-side (and it will seemingly move of its own volition) the baby-to-be is a boy; if it swings in a circle, the baby is a girl.

Answering Questions with a Pendulum

In a similar way, the pendulum will answer questions put to it, which can be about present problems or future outcomes, always providing that a 'Yes' or 'No' answer will suffice. For myself, 'Yes' is signified by a side-to-side movement and 'No' by a circular movement. But again, some dowsers find that the opposite is true for them. This being so, you should determine which direction represents 'Yes' or 'No' for you before you start asking questions. However, because the answers are coming from yourself (or perhaps 'through yourself' would be a better way of putting it) do remember that, when asking questions that concern yourself, your own hopes and expectations may influence the result. But this has not stopped some people from basing their business decisions on the swing of a pendulum. For example, Bruce Sullivan, a member of the board of trustees of the American Dowsers' Association, uses one as an executive decision-making tool for the analysis of markets, ideas and concepts. 'Let's say I'm approached by a particular distributor who wants to handle one of our products,' he explains, 'and who is located some distance away. If I don't have the time or the information to evaluate his operation by the usual methods, I can use the pendulum to assess his company's credibility, aggressiveness, and its ability to handle the product. It's basically the same as looking for water.'

Alternative Types of Rod

Many modern dowsers employ lengths of flexible metal wire, which are typically bent into a circle, as dowsing rods, or alternatively, they make use of two strips of plastic, which are tied together side-by-side at one end, in lieu of the traditional Y-shaped dowsing rod, although both are held in very much the same way.

Straight, Single Rods

Straight single rods, when used, are typically long, slender and tapering, and are held by the thinnest end, between the hands, to give their response by an up and down movement at their far end. Such rods are sometimes employed to find water and minerals, but they are perhaps more commonly used to determine depth. The operator first decides how many feet are symbolized by each bob of the stick. Let's say he decides that each one represents 10 ft (3 m). He then asks the stick how many feet down the object or substance is, and counts the number of bobs it makes. If it moves up and down twenty times before coming to rest, he knows that the prime depth of the target is 20 x 10 ft or 200 ft (60 m). Then, if he narrows down the depth scale to one bob equals one foot, and the rod in turn bobs six more times, he can say with exactitude that the target lies 206 ft (61.8 m) beneath the surface of the ground.

Manufactured Rods

Over the years a number of manufactured devices have come on to the market which are promoted as being improvements on the traditional ones. These often incorporate springs to amplify the dowsing effect, and some of them, like the 'Magnetomatic Locator' and the 'Aurameter', have been successfully used in the field (see Figure 7).

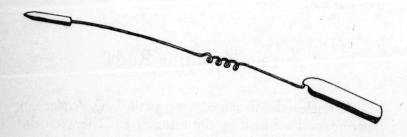

Figure 7: The 'Aurameter' dowsing rod.

Dowsing with the Hands

But some dowsers, remarkably enough, don't need to use a dowsing rod at all; their hands alone are sufficiently sensitive. They walk over the site to be investigated shaking their hands from side to side, and when they arrive at a spot where their hands stop shaking, seemingly of their own accord, they know that they have found their target. However, dowsing with bare hands is a fairly rare skill, so do experiment with a forked stick and a pendulum before trying it.

A few years ago Uri Geller, the psychic metal-bender, was advised by Sir Val Duncan, a former managing director of Rio Tinto and a dowser himself, that he would make more money by finding metal than by bending it. And Geller, interested by this proposition, took some lessons from Sir Val. He now sells his services for very large sums to anyone who wants help in finding metal ores, oil, or anything else, and while he does not claim to be 100 per cent accurate, the mining companies he largely works for are happy if his results are significantly better than they might otherwise expect. And Geller does not use a dowsing rod. Instead, like the Navaho 'hand tremblers', he finds what he is searching for by feel. He dowses, in other words, with his hands.

CHAPTER THREE

DOWSING
METHODS

And I will give thee the treasures of darkness,
and the hidden riches of secret places.

From Isaiah, XLV

Early Theories about Underground
Water Sources

When the Greek writer Plutarch described the expedition
mounted by the Roman Paulus Aemilius into his country, he
noted that at one stage the invaders ran very short of water,

> ... for only a little, and that but indifferent, flowed, or
> rather came drop by drop, from some springs near the
> sea. In this extremity, Aemilius, seeing Mount Olympus
> before him, very high and covered with trees,
> conjectured from their verdure, that there must be

springs in it which would discharge themselves at the bottom, and therefore caused several pits and wells to be dug at the foot of it. These were soon filled with clear water, which ran from them with great force and rapidity, because it had been confined there.[3]

The Roman adventurer did not employ dowsers to find the water for him, but instead surveyed the landscape in the manner of a modern geologist and determined from what he saw that water was likely to be found in the ground at the foot of the holy mountain. His actions would of course be applauded by scientists, because Aemilius was acting in a highly rational way, although we can be sure that had dowsing for water been known in the ancient world, he would surely have made use of it. But what follows perhaps provides us with a clue as to why the ancients did not learn to dowse.

Some, however, deny that there are any hidden sources constantly provided with water in the places from which it flows; nor will they allow the discharge to be owing to the opening of a vein; but they will have it, that the water is formed instantaneously, from the condensation of vapours, and that by the coldness and pressure of the earth a moist vapour is rendered fluid. For, as the breasts of women are not, like vessels, stored with milk always ready to flow, but prepare and change the nutriment that is in them into milk; so the cold and springy places in the ground, have not a quantity of water hid within them, which as from reservoirs always full, can be sufficient to supply large streams and rivers; but by compressing and condensing the vapours and the air, they convert them into water. And such places being opened, afford that element freely, just as the breasts of women do milk from their being sucked, by compressing and liquifying vapour; whereas the earth that remains idle and undug, cannot produce any water, because it wants that motion which alone is the true cause of it.

Thus some Greeks and Romans did not believe that there are underground sources of water worth digging for, but rather that such water, when it manifested, was produced by uprising vapours being compressed into a liquid at the site from which it flowed. Hence digging for water, from this theoretical standpoint, was a waste of time.

But Plutarch, evidently disagreeing, goes on to note that:

... those that teach this doctrine give occasion to the sceptical to observe, that by parity of reason there is no blood in animals, but that the wound produces it, by a change in the flesh and the spirits, which that impression renders fluid. Besides that doctrine is refuted by those who digging deep in the earth to undermine some fortification, or to search for metals, meet with deep rivers, not collected little by little, which would be the case if they were produced at the instant the earth were opened, but rushing upon them at once in great abundance. And it often happens upon the breaking of a great rock, that a quantity of water issues out, which as suddenly ceases.

Contemporary Theories

The modern dowser is similarly convinced of the reality of underground water, which he believes flows in channels or veins through the earth beneath him. Such veins sometimes slope upwards, so bringing water from a deeper level to a point quite close to the surface.

The hydrologist, by contrast, doubts the existence of water veins. For him, subsurface water is present because rainwater has soaked into the ground and accumulates when its downward passage is prevented by some impervious layer, such as clay. The upper surface of this accumulated mass of water is known as the water table, whose depth varies from place to place. In some areas, such as the London basin, it is comparatively near the surface, which means that wells can be dug down to it and water drawn from it; or, alternatively, if the valley containing the water table is steep sided and the water table itself is curved upwards by the stratum within which it lies, there may be sufficient pressure exerted by the curvature to force water upwards and thus out of the well or bore-hole.

But in accordance with Plutarch's observation that 'it often happens upon the breaking of a great rock, that a quantity of water issues out, which as suddenly ceases', there are now some geologists who believe that the bulk of subsurface water has not originated from rainwater soaking into the ground, but has instead been formed within the rocks themselves. In fact a paper published more than eighty years ago by the Swedish academic, Professor Adolf Nordenskiold, gives credence to this idea. Titled 'About Drilling for Water in Primary Rocks', the paper describes how water is created in crystalline rocks by a little understood process, from where it can be extracted by drilling operations. Equally enigmatic is the apparent upwelling of water into the cones of mountains and hills which brings it within drilling or digging distance of their summits. This remarkable phenomenon was taken advantage of in olden days, and is one of the reasons why so many forts, castles and other defensive dwellings were built on the tops of hills. And while 'the breaking of a great rock' can only give rise to 'a quantity of water ... which as suddenly ceases', the amount of water present within a rock stratum is often more than sufficient to give rise to a sustained flow of clear, good quality water capable of supplying the needs of a small settlement or town.

Dowsing and Global Warming

If the worst fears of climatologists are realized (and the droughts which have affected Britain during the last couple of years suggest that they might be) then the world, or at least parts of it, may soon suffer from a severe water shortage. Farmers will be particularly badly hit, and many may try to find water on their property by drilling bore-holes and wells, the siting of which can be most accurately pin-pointed by dowsing. So, if you have perhaps been wondering why it is worth learning to dowse if water is so readily available from our taps, take note of the steadily worsening climatic situation and remember: in a world with no water, the dowser is king!

Dowsing Your Own Garden

You may feel ready to test your own dowsing skills. If so, there is no reason why you shouldn't start in your own back garden by looking for an underground water vein (or veins), a water pipe, or an electricity cable. And in case you think that there is bound to be water if you dig down deep enough, it is worth pointing out that most dowsers are not sensitive to still or standing water, but only to water that is flowing, as it would be through a vein. The first thing you need to do is to cut yourself a dowsing rod from one of your apple trees or from another of the tree types mentioned earlier. Or, if you prefer, you can use a couple of L-rods cut from wire coat hangers.

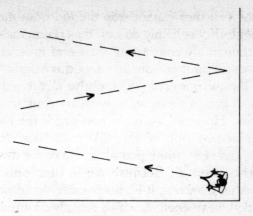

Figure 8: Dowsing a small plot.

When investigating a small area the size of the average back garden, you can just walk from side to side, in a zig zag motion, which will eventually take you from one end of the garden to the other. You set out, of course, from one corner of the garden, holding your rod as previously described. Keep your elbows close to your body, and make sure that your forearms are held our horizontally. Your grip on the arms of the Y-shaped rod should be sufficient to bend them outwards, which in turn imparts an incipient rotational movement to them (see Figure 8).

How the Rod Works

Tests have shown that the rod is actually moved by unconscious muscle contractions in the arms of the person holding it when the dowsing signal is received. The mystery of dowsing is not that the muscles play a part in the movement, but what it is that causes them to contract.

Dowsers say that they cannot stop the rod from moving, try as they might; they certainly do not, they claim, make the rod move by consciously contracting their arm muscles. For the moment we will limit our discussion of this enigma by saying only that the rod moves in response to a received dowsing signal, which brings about an involuntary contraction of the arm muscles. However, we must not ignore the fact, which was underlined by Bob Weeks, that many dowsers feel 'an undeniable and very strong pull of the tip of the divining rod towards the ground'. Because while this 'pull' may be apparent rather than real, it is also possible that dowsing may involve little-known energies which actually do attract the rod to the ground.

Choosing Your Target

I have already pointed out that dowsers can locate the position in the ground of all manner of things which are hidden and out of sight. The next question is, how do you distinguish between them? After all, you don't want to go out looking for water only to end up finding a buried electricity cable.

The answer is far less difficult than it might sound. All you need to do is to set out with a mental image of what you want to find. If you wish to locate water, for example, you set out with that intention and this will ensure that your dowsing rod moves only when you are over water. Similarly, if you want to locate the course of an electricity cable under your lawn, then you set out with the intention of finding it and this will be quite sufficient to prevent your rod from dipping when you cross, as you might, a water pipe.

However, some dowsers are really 'water-diviners' in the

sense that they cannot find anything else: Bob Weeks is such a man (as is Michael Cranfield, who we shall meet later). But you might not be so circumscribed. Only experience will tell you if you are or not.

Tracing a Water Pipe

Let us imagine that you want to trace the course of a water pipe under your lawn, which may run as shown in Figure 9. You start out as previously described; but you should not stop and shout 'Eureka' when you get a positive dowsing response at position A, but rather mark the site with a peg and then continue striding out the whole of the lawn or yard with your

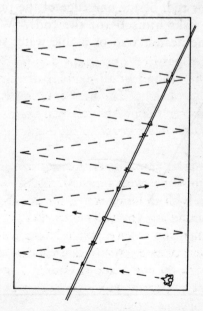

Figure 9: How to trace the course of a waterpipe.

dowsing rod. You mark each place where the rod subsequently dips with another peg, so that by the time you have reached the far end of the lawn or yard you will have left a line of pegs that mark the route of the water pipe (or electricity cable, or whatever else you are searching for).

Investigating a Large Area

It is fine to investigate a small plot of land in this way but this method becomes too tedious and time-consuming when the area is large — and some properties are several hundred acres in size. With such properties it is necessary to narrow down the search area. One way of doing this is for the dowser to stand, with his rod, beside one edge of the property, facing along it. He asks himself (or the rod), 'Where on this property is the nearest vein of usable water situated?', and

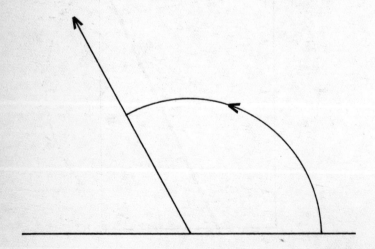

Figure 10: Turning through a semi-circle to find direction of target.

then slowly begins to turn through a semi-circle. When he reaches the spot where the rod is pointing towards the vein, he should get a normal dowsing response, i.e. the rod will dip downwards. He thus knows the line on which the water vein lies relative to his position (see Figure 10).

How Far Away is the Water Vein?

He now needs to know how far away from him the vein is. To discover this he re-positions his rod and asks, 'How far from me is the water vein? 10 feet? 20 feet? 30 feet? 40 feet? 50 feet?' etc. Let's say the vein lies 110 ft (33 m) from him.

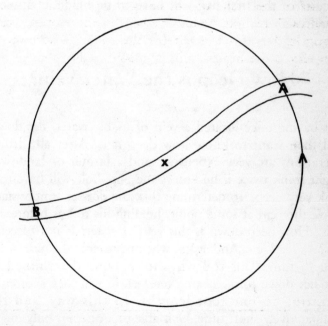

Figure 11: Method of plotting the course of a water vein.

When he counts to 110 ft (33 m), his rod will again dip, indicating that the vein lies this distance from him.

Two important co-ordinates have now been obtained: the line on which the water vein is situated and its distance away. He need only follow that line the requisite number of feet to obtain a further reaction from his rod, which verifies the vein's presence. He will then mark the spot with a peg. Should he next wish to identify the underground course of the vein, he simply moves 30 ft (9 m) or 40 ft (12 m) from the peg and walks around it in a circle, holding his dowsing rod as before. The rod will again dip when he crosses the vein, first at site A in Figure 11, and secondly at site B, both of which are also marked with pegs. Together, the three pegs mark the vein's approximate line of flow. If greater accuracy is required, more circuits of the first peg will have to be made at different distances.

How Deep is the Water Vein?

But having once located a vein of usable water, the dowser will then want to know how deep it is. After all, drilling operations are very expensive, and a farmer or landowner might think twice if he knows the bore-hole will have to be sunk very deep. To determine this, the dowser simply stands above the vein at some point, holding his rod as before, and asks, 'How deep down is this vein of water? Is it 10 feet? 20 feet? 30 feet?' etc. And again, when he reaches the nearest ten-foot distance, his rod will dip. Having determined the distance down to the nearest ten feet, he can then shorten his counting to one-foot lengths. In this way, and in a comparatively short time, he is able to locate not only the site of the water vein, but also its course and depth.

Establishing Depth using Bishop's Rule

Another useful method of determining depth is the so-called Bishop's Rule, which is named after the Bishop of Grenoble, in France, who tested the amazing dowsing abilities of Barthelemy Bléton in the eighteenth century. It can be summarized as 'the distance out equals the distance down' (see Figure 12).

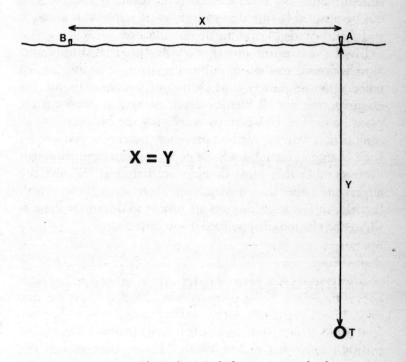

Figure 12: The Bishop's Rule for estimating depth.

Here is what you do. Having once located the point (or points) beneath which your target lies, mark its position with a peg.

Now stand over the peg, relax for a few moments, and then raise your dowsing rod(s) to the operative position and concentrate on the target's depth. Next, walk slowly away from the peg and keep walking until you get a dowsing response from your rod(s). Mark the place with another peg. The distance between the two pegs represents the depth of the target.

Then return to the first peg and repeat the procedure by heading in another direction. Do this perhaps two or three times. You should find that you get a dowsing response at approximately the same distance each time. If you do, you can be reasonably sure that your dowsing response is accurate and that the target lies at the depth indicated.

But I must point out that while this is a simple and straightforward method of estimating depth, it should not be relied upon absolutely. The Bishop of Grenoble found, for example, that not all Bléton's depth estimations were correct when he used it. However, by employing the Bishop's Rule in conjunction with the method previously described, you stand a good chance of getting a reliable depth measurement, although do remember that most dowsers are better at locating the target's site rather than its depth or, where water is concerned, its yield. In fact some dowsers are unable to determine these at all, so don't be too disappointed if you can't either.

Estimating the Yield of a Water Vein

The yield of a water vein can be estimated by again repositioning your rod and asking, 'How many gallons per minute flow will this vein give? Will it yield 10 gallons? 20? 30? 40?' and so on, until the rod dips downwards, indicating the rate of flow that can be expected. Questions can also be put to the rod regarding the water's purity, if necessary, such as 'Is this water drinkable?' and 'Is this water clear and unpolluted?' Pure water is obviously required for drinking but if the object of the exercise is to provide water for, say, irrigation, then it is not so important for the outflow to be completely free of dissolved minerals, which while perhaps harmless in themselves might give the water an unfortunate colour or a disagreeable taste.

Map Dowsing

The field-dowsing operations described are suitable for relatively small areas of land. For investigating the potential of much larger acreages, it is best to narrow down the area to be field dowsed by determining the probable site of a water vein (or oil well, ore body, missing person, etc) on a map. Map dowsing has been used for many years and is indeed an essential adjuvant of the dowser's art. It is particularly useful when a dowser is asked to find water or whatever in remote areas or in those that are difficult to traverse.

Triangulation

Map dowsing is most successfully done with a pendulum. The prime technique employed is called triangulation. For this you require a pendulum and also a small-scale map of the entire area of your operation. You begin by asking the pendulum (or your dowsing rod, if you prefer) if a steady supply of drinkable water (or whatever) is present anywhere below ground in the area of land represented by the map. For myself, if the pendulum swings to and fro, the answer is Yes;

if it swings in a circle, the answer is No. (These directions of swing may, however, be different for you, as some dowsers find that a side-to-side movement represents a negative response, whilst a circular movement represents a positive response.)

If you get a Yes response, move next to one of the bottom corners of the map. Position your elbow on the table to steady the hand holding the pendulum and then ask: 'In which direction does the nearest water vein lie?' When the pendulum starts to swing steadily to and fro, take a ruler in your other hand and line up one edge of it with the swing line of the pendulum across the map. Then draw a pencil line on the map along the edge of the ruler. Next, move your pendulum arm to the opposite bottom corner of the map and repeat the procedure, so that you end up with a second pencil line crossing the first. The site of the water vein (or whatever it is you are looking for) is indicated by the point at which the lines cross (see Figure 13).

If you start with a relatively small-scale map (such as the Ordnance Survey one inch to the mile) the point at which the lines cross will only give you an approximate position for the water vein. To identify the particular field in which it lies, or even the exact site in the field, you should then take a large-scale map of the area (like the Ordnance Survey six inches to the mile) and do the same thing again. Once you have narrowed down your search in this way, you can then walk or drive to the actual site and verify your findings (or not, as the case may be) with your dowsing rod.

Some dowsers prefer to use a more laborious pendulum technique where maps are concerned. This involves going over the map from side-to-side with a pendulum, watching for it to swing, which it usually does in a circular motion if water, for example, is indicated. This procedure is made less time-consuming if the client can say where he would like water to be found, if available, as the dowser can start testing at that point and need only look further afield if he does not get a positive response.

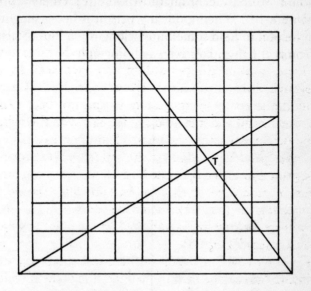

Figure 13: Plotting the location of a target (T) by triangulation on a map.

Map dowsing can in theory be used to locate anything, from veins of water and mineral deposits to missing persons and lost jewellery.

Using 'Witnesses'

Many dowsers like to hold a small sample of the substance being sought to help them 'tune in' to its position on a map or in the field. Such samples are colloquially termed 'witnesses'. When a liquid like water or oil is being sought, it is usual to put a few c.c.s in a small bottle and to hold that. Or alternatively, the bottle can be used as a plumb-bob and suspended at the end of a piece of cotton or string, which is then employed as an ordinary pendulum for map work, etc (see Figure 14). When a missing person is being sought, it is often helpful to hold something belonging to him or her such as a comb or hairgrip, or even a photograph.

Figure 14: A liquid 'witness' used as a pendulum.

The dowsing techniques outlined above should give you sufficient information to get started in this fascinating business. Later you will gradually develop your own methods and idiosyncrasies, for just as each person is different, so too is every dowser; and after all, it isn't the method that matters so much as the result.

CHAPTER FOUR

HOW DOWSING WORKS

A wise man endeavours, by considering all circumstances, to make conjectures, and form conclusions.

From *Thoughts on Various Subjects, Moral and Diverting* by Jonathan Swift

Dowsers do find what they are looking for. Thousands of water sources, oil deposits, and mineral lodes, plus all manner of lost objects and numerous missing persons, have been located by dowsers in Britain, the United States, and in most other parts of the world. This has been accomplished using the methods previously outlined, and also, amazingly enough, by dowsers operating from automobiles and even from aeroplanes. The latter are typically used to investigate remote or inaccessible terrain, or areas for which accurate maps are not available. Most aerial dowsing has taken place above the virgin outback of the USSR. And in one experiment carried out by the Soviet researcher Nikolai Sochevanov, dowsers working in an aeroplane were able to locate a 3 ft (90 cm) thick lead seam lying 500 ft (150m) underground.

Yet if dowsing does work, it is pertinent and necessary to ask how: how can a man or woman armed with nothing more than a forked stick find objects or substances that may be buried many hundreds of feet below the surface of the ground? And that's not all; 'A good dowser,' claimed Bruce Sullivan when I interviewed him in Canada, 'can determine the direction of the water flow, its depth, and give a reliable estimate of its volume and pressure. And a very skilled dowser can tell if the water is drinkable or not. He is also able to give similar information about buried oil or mineral deposits.'

But just by asking the question, we are stepping into something of a minefield. There are numerous hypotheses to account for the success of dowsing, ranging from outright fraud to the weird and the wonderful. Here I can do no more than consider the most credible of them. Let us start at the beginning.

The Movement of the Rod

The dowser, working in the field, feels a distinct and often powerful 'pull' on his divining rod when he reaches the site of the underground water vein or whatever. This 'pull', as I have already noted, may be sufficient to twist the arms of the rod within its bark, or sometimes to actually break them. Its dramatic nature is quite enough to convince many dowsers that there is an actual attractive force generated between the rod and the hidden target, which they often liken to that between a powerful magnet and a piece of iron. But if this were true, it would surely mean that not only could anyone become a good dowser, but that all dowsers should be equally proficient. This, however, is not the case. For among practising dowsers the talent manifests, like all human talents, on a sliding scale ranging from 'quite good' to 'excellent'. And even more mysteriously, some dowsers can only find water, while others can find anything with equal facility.

Unconscious Muscular Contraction

In fact the movement of the dowsing rod is best explained by unconscious muscular contraction in the arms of the dowser which directs the rod downwards or, as sometimes occurs, upwards. I have already described how the dowser, by gripping the rod in the prescribed manner, imparts an 'incipient rotational impetus' to it, which derives from the outward bending of the rod's springy arms. If the initial balance is then upset by a tightening of the arm muscles, the rod will flick downwards with sufficient force to perhaps twist the wood inside the bark at the points where it is held. The dowser, of course, is not aware of any such contraction occurring in his arm muscles, and may deny that it takes place at all, but the contractions need only be slight to unbalance what is, after all, an unstable system.

If unconscious muscle action sounds a somewhat suspect concept, it should be pointed out that we have a whole range of muscles that work, contracting and relaxing, day in, day out, without us being aware of their doing so at all. The muscles in the wall of the oesophagus, the stomach, the small intestine, and the large intestine, whose function is to move the food that we eat along the length of the alimentary canal, function in this way. So do the muscles of the heart. Likewise, the muscles of the eyelids, while they can be consciously contracted and relaxed, normally do so 'on their own' — i.e.

unconsciously — several times a minute, so causing us to blink, a movement which spreads the lachrymal fluid or tears over the surface of the eyes to keep them moist. And we all know that when we accidentally pick up something hot, unconscious reflex action makes us drop it immediately.

It was the physiologist W. B. Carpenter who first suggested that ideas could bring about unconscious muscle activity. In his celebrated paper 'On the Influence of Suggestion in Modifying and Directing Muscular Movement, Independently of Volition' (1852) he noted that:

> ... ideas may become the sources of muscular movement, independently either of volitions or of emotions ... thus, the ideo-motor principle of action finds its appropriate place in the physiological scale, which would, indeed, be incomplete without it.

Such non-volitional or unconscious muscle activity, which has been brought about by an idea or intention, takes place nearly every time we tie our shoelaces, write a letter, ride a bicycle, or do anything else that we don't have to think about. And similarly, dowsing is an ideomotor response: the dowser sets out with the intention or idea of finding water (or whatever) by means of his divining rod, which he believes will respond by turning downwards (or upwards) when he finds it. Thus the dowser in this sense is primed, and his muscles will unconsciously contract and so turn the rod when the 'correct spot' is located.

Tremor

There is another type of unconscious muscle movement known as *tremor*, which is responsible for the movement of a pendulum when you hold it between your thumb and forefinger. You can most easily detect tremor in yourself by extending your arm and holding your hand still: it won't be long before you notice a slight (or perhaps not so slight) shaking of your fingers. Dr Martin Lakie of the Department of Biology at St Andrews University, Scotland, aided by a grant from the Wellcome Trust, has been investigating tremor, and I travelled up to talk to him about his research.

'Everyone has tremor,' he told me. 'Although you may not be able to see it, your hands and other parts of your body are continuously in motion. The movements are very small, but with suitable instruments we can record it. And one of the striking things about it is the frequency at which it occurs is remarkably constant, usually between 8 and 11 cycles per second in everyone. What is not so constant is the amount. In any one individual the amount can vary from day-to-day by a factor of 3. And between individuals the amount can vary much more, perhaps over a range of a hundred fold.'

Dr Lakie's measurements of tremor are carried out as illustrated in Figure 15. The subject sits with both wrists unsupported, and two accelerometers, which detect the movement, such as it is, at the wrist joint, are separately attached to the middle finger of each hand. The signals are fed into and recorded by a computer-based analysis system and later analysed. The tremor of both hands is recorded for 80 seconds, which enables Dr Lakie to obtain a comprehensive picture of the tremor of the subject at that time.

Men tend to have a slightly larger amount of tremor on average than women, which perhaps explains why they are rather better at dowsing with a pendulum. And interestingly, when Dr Lakie recorded my tremor rates while I held my pendulum and put two questions to it (one evoking a negative, the other a positive, response), we found that my tremor increased to provide the motive force which moved the pendulum.

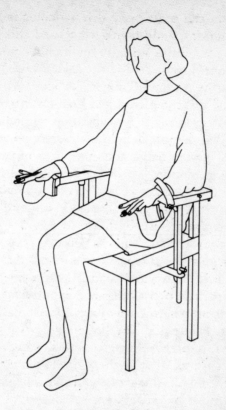

Figure 15: Dr Lakie's method of investigating tremor.

'The difference wasn't enormous between the negative circling movements of the pendulum and the positive side-to-side movements,' noted Dr Lakie, 'but there was a clear difference between the pendulum at rest and when it was making these movements. There was more tremor present when the pendulum was moving than when it wasn't. But we weren't able to distinguish between what made the pendulum move in a rotary manner and what made it move in a linear manner. Perhaps more sensitive equipment is required to do this.'

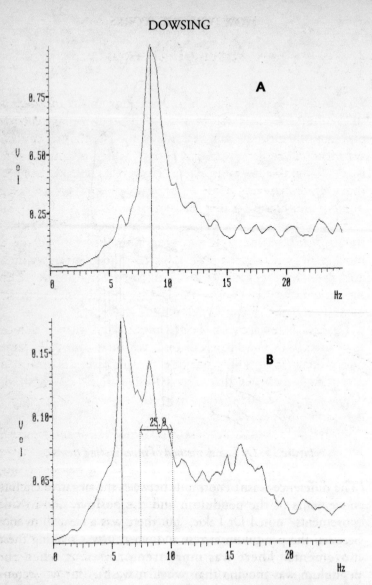

Figure 16: Graph A shows normal tremor in author's right hand; Graph B shows increased tremor while author holds a pendulum and puts a question to it.

Causes of Tremor

The cause of tremor, which is an oscillation in the muscles, is still not understood. It has been suggested that it is a 'feedback problem' affecting the muscles, due to the fact that all control systems oscillate if they are not perfect, which of course none is, so all 'tremble' to some extent. However, Dr Lakie believes that tremor happens because the muscles consist of a large number of motor units that act asynchronously.

'The motor units fire off and they produce a little "kick",' he explains, 'and what you get when they produce a movement is a summation of all these little "kicks", which add together to give a fairly smooth movement. The movement of course is not entirely smooth, because it consists of all these little "kicks", which result in tremor.'

Dr Lakie's research has been concentrated on the tremor associated with Parkinson's disease, which is unusually large and often of a very low frequency. Parkinson's disease is a progressive disorder that may take ten or fifteen years to develop, and he hopes that his work may lead to an earlier detection of the condition.

'We've been measuring tremor in a large number of normal subjects and also in a large number of subjects whom we consider, for one reason or another, may be at risk of getting Parkinson's disease. It's known, for example, that certain drugs predispose a patient to getting Parkinson's disease. And we've been able to show that if you make measurements in this way you can pick up tremors that are not actually obvious to the condition, but which may forewarn of its development. We've also found that people under stress have a higher tremor, and that some occupational groups have more tremor than others.'

It has been shown that caffeine produces an increase in tremor while alcohol reduces it, at least in the short term. Dr Lakie remarked that anyone who has played darts or snooker knows that his or her performance is improved by drinking a couple of pints, and he thinks that it is no coincidence that professional darts and snooker players tend to be fairly heavy drinkers.

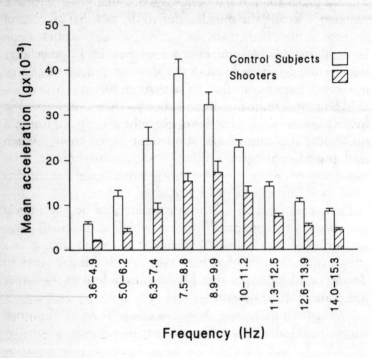

Figure 17: Graph showing low tremor rates of shooters.

He is also interested in the fine control of tremor, and has found that people who shoot, for example, are capable of holding their limbs very still. He has made measurements of tremor in elite Olympic standard shooters and discovered that their tremor levels are rather low, as the graph in Figure 17 shows. 'But whether they have low tremor levels and therefore become shooters,' he says, 'or whether they become shooters and then learn how to suppress their tremor is another question. We don't know the answer to that.'

What Causes Accurate Responses?

Yet while we can be reasonably, if not absolutely, certain that it is the dowser who causes his divining rod (or pendulum) to move, we must now consider why it moves when it does. What, in other words, causes his muscles to contract over the spot where the water or other target substance lies? There are three principal hypotheses to account for this, which are considered below.

The Response to Visual Clues Hypothesis

The proponents of this hypothesis point out that most dowsers work in terrain that they know well and whose subsurface potential, with regard to water, oil, iron ore or whatever, is broadly understood. They further assume that whatever is below ground produces some change, however slight, at the surface. For example, the presence of a water vein may be revealed by the faster growth of plants, or by the growth of different plants, above it. And the dowser, they say, simply responds, albeit unconsciously, to these visual clues, whose reception causes an ideomotor response in his arm muscles, which dips the rod downwards and thus identifies the site of the water or whatever.

That dowsers may, at least on occasion, respond to visual clues, is suggested by the experience of Bob Weeks, who told me:

'I once had the experience of passing over an area where there was not thought to be, or known to be, water — it was on my father's property and I had asked him about it but he knew of none — and I got a very strong pull from the divining rod. Now I'm not particularly observant of things and it was only after I'd gone back or forth over the area several times that I realized that the vegetation was slightly different. It was in a mown area but there were plants — I don't know what they were — growing close to the ground among the grasses, which didn't grow anywhere else. And I can only assume that they had something to do with the supply of water beneath the ground.'

Bob also agreed that his father, a successful amateur dowser, worked in areas that he knew well, saying: 'Dad had grown up in Vermont and so he knew the landscape — and there are a lot of streams and water-course ways in the Vermont landscape — and I'm sure he may have had a feeling or a suspicion where he might find water. But he also mentioned to me how often he would be surprised by finding it where he didn't really expect it to be.'

The Psychic Hypothesis

The supporters of this hypothesis make the point that while visual clues, subliminally perceived, may aid dowsers in the field, they cannot possibly explain all successful dowsing attempts and certainly not those performed with a map and a pendulum. And while the reader may protest that a detailed Ordnance survey map can provide clues to the trained eye as to what lies beneath the surface of the area in question, few dowsers, if any, have the detailed knowledge to interpret a map in this way, even if they wanted to. Furthermore, dowsers have been successful in dowsing from maps that are little more than rough sketches, and from which, by no stretch of the imagination, could they gain any useful knowledge, consciously or unconsciously, of what lay beneath the surface of the area they represented.

So an explanation of both map dowsing and field dowsing is that our minds have certain psychic abilities which give us information about our environment in ways that are quite different from those provided by our five familiar senses of sight, hearing, touch, taste, and smell. The most important psychic sense here is *clairvoyance*, which enables the mind to gain information directly about its surroundings. There is now a wealth of anecdotal and scientific evidence to support the reality of these apparently supernatural, but in fact very natural, psychic perceptions, and the interested reader may care to consult my book *The ESP Workbook* for a full account of them.

The dowser, according to this hypothesis, learns of the presence of water, or oil, or a mineral lode, etc, by detecting it at a subliminal level, clairvoyantly, when he either works his pendulum over a map or walks with his divining rod across the ground. The clairvoyantly-received information then acts as a 'dowsing signal' and prompts an ideomotor response in his arm muscles, which in turn causes the pendulum to swing in a particular direction, or the rod to turn downwards, thus identifying the location of the hidden target.

If true, this hypothesis explains why dowsers are sometimes wrong, because our psychic abilities do not function as well as our ordinary senses. Indeed, for reasons that are far from clear, they fluctuate, so that while they can be quite sharp and accurate on one day, they may function below par on another. But it is known that our perception or receptivity is affected by several factors. First, our physical state — fatigue and pain, for example, seem to inhibit it; second, our mood — our psychic awareness is greatest when we are relaxed and happy;

third, our ingestion of mild stimulants like caffeine, nicotine and, in moderate quantities, alcohol, which promote it; and fourth, the presence in the air of positive or negative ions. Positive ions, which are typically found in higher concentrations in the air on close, thundery days, depress psychic perceptivity, while negative ions, which interestingly accumulate in the air in the vicinity of running water, and when the day is bright and clear, especially after a rain shower, tend to bolster it.

But this hypothesis, while seemingly reasonable, is rejected by many dowsers, who prefer to believe that some mysterious force actually pulls their divining rod towards the ground, and by most official dowsing bodies. In fact I received a somewhat frosty reception when I telephoned the British Society of Dowsers for information about the current state of dowsing in Britain and revealed that the series of which this book forms a part includes such titles as *How To Be A Medium*, *Understanding Astral Projection*, and *How To Develop Your ESP*. 'Oh,' gasped the secretary, 'dowsing has nothing to do with them!' In other words, those activities are concerned with the 'supernatural', whereas dowsing, so long derided as a wacky pursuit engaged in by ignorant country folk, is an entirely rational, even scientifically-respectable, activity. Talk about the pot calling the kettle black!

The Electromagnetic Hypothesis

Dowsers frequently talk in rather vague terms about 'electricity' and 'magnetism' as being the forces which cause their divining rods to dip earthwards, despite the fact that they know, when questioned about it, that a magnet, even an electromagnet, will only attract iron to itself, not wood or plastic, which are the materials from which most dowsing rods are made; and even when the iron hoop which some dowsers favour is used, the strength of a magnetic field needed to draw it downwards, often against the muscular 'resistance' of the dowser, would be impossibly great.

But although it is unlikely that magnetism is directly responsible for pulling the dowsing rod towards the ground, recent research has shown that dowsers may be responding to minute variations in the magnetic field emanating from the earth beneath their feet.

Case Study 1

For example, the Czechoslovakian physicist Dr Zaboj Harvalik, who had long been interested in dowsing, decided to test dowsers to see if they are sensitive to electromagnetic waves. In one experiment he knocked two short lengths of metal pipe into the ground, 60 ft (18 m) apart, and connected them by wire to a battery. When the current was switched on, it ran through the earth from the negatively-charged pipe to the positively-charged pipe, thereby producing a magnetic field above the ground beneath them. As Harvalik was able to vary the strength of the electric current from between 0 and 150 milliamperes, he was thus able to vary the strength of the magnetic field.

He then had dowsers holding metal L-rods walk between the two pipes, and discovered that not only would the rods invariably swing outwards when they did so, thus indicating a response to the magnetic field, but that those who were very sensitive could detect it when the current strength was reduced to 0.5 milliamperes.

Harvalik next concentrated on trying to find the location of the magnetic sensors within the human body. He did this by covering different parts of the dowsers' bodies with *mu*-metal, a special alloy that is impermeable to a magnetic field, and discovered that when the waist area and the upper head region were thus protected, the dowser became insensitive to the presence of a magnetic field. Further research led him to identify the adrenal glands, which sit atop the kidneys, and the pituitary and/or the pineal gland of the head as being the likeliest sites of the human magnetic sensors.

Magnetic Variations

Local variations in the earth's magnetic field are produced by water flowing through underground channels, by man-made cavities such as mine tunnels and pipes, by living organisms, and by the different magnetic properties of mineral lodes, oil deposits and archaeological artefacts compared with that of the surrounding soil. The detection of these magnetic variations by the dowser acts as the dowsing signal, which in turn causes an ideomotor response of his arm muscles, thus dipping (or raising) the dowsing rod. Hence it appears that the human body does possess a genuine sixth sense, that of sensitivity to magnetic variations, which may perhaps explain why some people cannot sleep in certain rooms of a house or why particular houses have a depressing effect on their spirits. They are reacting negatively to the lines of magnetic force rising up from beneath them.

Map Dowsing

But while the electromagnetic hypothesis may well explain, or at least partly explain, how a dowser functions in the field, it cannot be the answer to map dowsing. There are no magnetic variations on the surface of a map. Hence map dowsing may call upon the dowser's psychic powers, which of course may also be employed, possibly in a secondary role, in field dowsing. After all, as Bruce Sullivan pointed out, the good dowser is not only able to locate the site of an underground water vein, but can 'determine the direction of water flow, its depth, and give a reliable estimate of its volume and pressure. And a very sensitive dowser can tell if the water is drinkable or not. He is also able to give similar information about buried oil and mineral deposits.' It is difficult to understand how all this information could be obtained from simple magnetic variations. Nor does it explain how the dowser is able to distinguish between a buried water pipe, a telephone cable, and an electricity cable, for example, if he is trying to find the telephone cable. These may well produce a different magnetic field, but how does he *know* which is which? For while he may be able instinctively to 'tune-in' to the presence of water, which is a biological necessity and thus something for which he may have been programmed by evolution, it is ridiculous to suppose that he has been similarly programmed to find modern artefacts like buried cables.

Case Study 2

Even more enigmatic are the observations made by the well-known Canadian scientist Dr Bernard Grad, a disciple of the late Wilhelm Reich. Grad found, while carrying out a number of as-yet unpublished experiments with the Quebec dowser Romunald Morin, in which he detected the production of electrical charges by Morin, that the dowsing rod which Morin held, contrary to the usual direction of movement, turned *towards* his body when he located the object or substance for which he was searching.

'Morin had a very, very interesting reaction to the dowsing signal. It was quite unique,' says Dr Grad, 'and he would get this reaction whether he was on the spot or dowsing from a map. He would use a forked piece of wood which he had himself designed, and upon receiving the dowsing signal he would get a powerful drawing of the stick to himself. It wasn't a gentle thing: it was really quick and very strong. And as a matter of fact, during that short period of time, you could actually hear the discharge of static electricity. He would also have two fellows, each with a pair of pliers, hold each side of the forked stick while he held it in his hands, and he would tell them to try and prevent the stick from being drawn to his body. But they could never stop it. And he was a man in his late 70s at the time! This would happen even if he was dowsing from a map. And for an instant the men couldn't even move the rod away from his shirt. Indeed, once he got an extremely long, flexible stick to bend towards him, even against his actions.

'I think that the body, in his case at least, develops a powerful charge, which induces an opposite charge into the stick that he's holding, so that it's attracted to him. There's no doubt that this is a reaction of the body itself. It can acquire strong charges — strong, electrical energy charges — and the rod can either be induced to move towards it or away from it. Hence the dowsing signal may not be visual, it may not be psychic, it may actually be *physical*. But I know there are supposed to be movements of the muscles as well, and I think these are valid too.'

To further complicate the issue, there are some dowsers who believe that they are responding to mysterious radiations or energy fields which are emitted by all bodies, including the human body. Their existence was first postulated by a Swiss priest, Abbé Alexis Mermet, who discovered that he could accurately diagnose illness with a pendulum, an art he termed 'radiesthesia'. But even more curious was the fact that the Abbé did not need to dowse over patients, as perhaps might be expected if he was responding to 'rays' given out by them, but could diagnose what was wrong from a distance of several miles.

This brings us to the field of medical dowsing, which is the subject of the next chapter. Prepare yourself for some surprises: the water is about to get a good deal muddier.

CHAPTER FIVE

MEDICAL DOWSING

The point is, with healing and, I think, with
dowsing too, that almost everyone who approaches
the thing tends to get caught up in a mystery —
and this aura of mystery can act as a block in
trying to see the fundamental truth of it.

Dr Bernard Grad

Almost one hundred years ago it was realized that, if dowsers
can locate the sites of water, oil, metals and other substances
or objects hidden in the ground, then similarly they ought to
be able to find the sites of disease in the human body. Tests
were therefore carried out, notably in France, and it was
discovered that they could. And it was later shown that
dowsing could also be used to determine what treatment was
most effective against the disease. This early work led to the
modern and comparatively widespread art of medical
dowsing.

Healing by Laying-on-of-hands

The reader may be familiar with healing by the laying-on-of-hands. Such healers cure by applying their hands to the afflicted body part, either directly or by holding them very close to the skin surface. It is an ancient form of alternative medicine, and indeed Jesus Christ himself often healed the sick in this way. St Mark tells us, for example, that when a leper came to him, Jesus 'put forth his hand, and touched him, and saith unto him ... be thou clean. And as soon as he had spoken, immediately the leprosy departed from him, and he was cleansed.'

Many who heal in this way can also detect the site of illness with their hands. 'As a rule,' notes Dr Bernard Grad, 'when healers lay their hands on you, they'll tell you of sensations they feel in their hands. These involve a sense of vibration, a sense of something moving in them, a sense of heat. They're actual signals which they get from the patient. Healers, in this regard, are dowsers.'

Such healers resemble those few field dowsers who do not need a dowsing rod but use only their hands. Most medical dowsers, however, are not so sensitive. They need a dowsing device with which to work, and the instrument of their choice is the pendulum.

Case Study 1: Romunald Morin

It was a pendulum that the Quebec dowser Romunald Morin used in an important, but as yet unpublished, experiment conducted by Dr Grad under laboratory conditions. It is worth considering in some detail because it says much about the validity of dowsing and about the nature of the disease signal to which the dowser responds.

Dr Grad bred two strains of white laboratory mice. One strain consisted of normal, healthy mice; the other of mice that spontaneously developed leukaemia. The onset of leukaemia in the latter strain was made evident by the mice's hunched appearance, the greying of their hair, and their laboured respiration. They also developed enlarged lymph nodes.

Dr Grad then took five large, opaque paper bags. Into four of them he put a healthy mouse, while into the fifth he put a sick mouse. The bags were then closed. He then had Romunald Morin try to find which bag held the sick mouse by dowsing for it.

'We began the experiment,' explained Dr Grad, by bringing the bags into a room, lining them up, and having Morin go by with his pendulum and try to pick out the bag with the sick mouse in it. He carried a "witness" with him that consisted of the organs of a mouse that had died from leukaemia. Then, when he pointed out the bag he thought the target was in, it was opened and the result recorded.'

Because the assistant who brought the bags into the room and lined them up did not know which bag held the sick mouse, the experiment was double-blind. However, it was found that Morin, as he worked his way along the row of bags, tended to identify the bag immediately before the one with the sick mouse in it as the target bag.

'Let's say the sick animal was in bag number 4,' said Dr Grad. 'Yet when Morin was passing bag number 3 he would start to get a signal and he would think that (the sick mouse) was in that bag. So we would take out the mouse and see that it was normal. Then we would have him test again and he'd say, "No, it's in bag number 4." So we decided that we would bring in each bag separately and have him test one at a time. And later on he tested for the sick mouse from another room, and on at least one occasion he tested for it from his house, which was five or six miles away.'

Altogether Morin tried to find the sick mouse a total of 19 times. This meant that chance alone would have allowed him to correctly identify it on four occasions.

'But counting all the experiments, including those in which the bags were in a line, he was actually correct 12 times,' noted Dr Grad. 'And where he missed, he almost every time got it right on the next shot.'

The experiment showed that a dowser can locate a diseased target, in this case a sick mouse, with a success rate well above chance. But Morin's failures are equally interesting because they suggest that the sick animal was producing some type of energy field which radiated out around it, causing a response in the dowser prematurely and misleading him into thinking that the bag lying immediately before it was the right one.

Pin-pointing the Site of an Illness

Many dowsers would say that the last paragraph could be suitably amended to 'the sick animal was producing some type of *negative* energy field which radiated out around it', as they believe that all things, both living and non-living, give out an energy field. Yet even this notion can be refined because a medical dowser can not only tell if an animal is ill, but which organ or part of it is injured or diseased. This implies that the negative radiation is concentrated on, and spreads out from, the diseased part. Indeed, the rest of the animal (or person) may be quite healthy and thus continues to emit a positive radiation.

However, there is as yet no scientific evidence that either

living or non-living things produce energy fields of the type described, so they may be entirely imaginary. It may also mean, of course, that only the human body is sensitive enough to detect them.

Abbé Alexis Mermet

Medical dowsing was first practised by a French priest named Abbé Alexis Mermet who, after successfully using a pendulum to locate water and other substances hidden in the ground, decided to apply the technique to the bodies of sick people and animals. He went on to enjoy great renown as a diagnostician, and concluded that he was responding to some change in the energy field produced by his patients. This later led another priest, Abbé Alexis Bouly, to call the method *radiesthesia*, which means 'the perception of radiations'.

Dowsing and Homoeopathy

But medical dowsers not only diagnose, they also treat the sick. In fact they are often able to cure patients who have been given up as hopeless cases by their conventionally-trained physicians. To do so, many employ homoeopathic remedies, the most effective being chosen by dowsing for it with a pendulum from a list of those known to be beneficial for the condition. This means, of course, that they must use extra-sensory perception to select the best remedy, as a list of printed or written names cannot itself be giving out radiations of different strengths. Yet once the actual remedy has been taken down from the shelf its potential can be verified by the dowser using his pendulum, which may mean that its energy field, if it exists, is being responded to directly.

Homoeopathy was invented by Christian Samuel Hahnemann (1755–1843), who discovered that if patients are given minute doses of a substance which would, in large doses, produce similar symptoms to those of the disease from which they are suffering, it would effect a cure. Thus Hahnemann let the symptoms guide or even dictate the cure, whereas conventional doctors use the symptoms merely for diagnosis and thereafter ignore them, except in so far as their disappearance shows them that the treatment they have prescribed is working.

Dowsing and Healing by Colour

Another alternative form of treatment sometimes used by medical dowsers is healing by colour. This involves correcting a vibrational imbalance of the body by mentally projecting into it a particular colour or colours. One of Britain's foremost colour healers is Ronald Leech, who runs a clinic at Bexhill, Sussex. He told me:

'Each part of the body vibrates at a different rate, so that to have a body in complete harmony you have to have all the organs vibrating at their correct rate. If there's a wrong vibration, one must apply a vibration at either a higher or lower rate to correct the trouble. And the easiest way of doing this is by colour. Colour is a vibration, and one offsets the disharmonies by mentally applying a colour.'

Leech says that colour healing is not used to treat infectious diseases, which are most effectively dealt with by conventional medicine, but those resulting from stress and bodily degeneration. It is widely used, for example, to counteract anxiety and depression, migraine headaches, insomnia, and muscle pains, as well as more serious disorders like arthritis, rheumatism, and heart ailments.

'There are specific colours which give particular actions on different parts of the body,' he explains. 'For example, if we wanted to calm a person's nerves — a person who is very upset — we would use sapphire blue, and we would apply it to the solar plexus. This is done by mentally picturing sapphire blue and directing it into the solar plexus by placing our fingertips, or even the palms of the hands, on that part of the person's body.'

Bright colours like gold and orange are typically used to cheer people up and to restore confidence. Violet and amethyst are both used to treat certain heart complaints. However, the two most widely used healing colours are spring green and sapphire blue, whose vibrations have both a healing and soothing effect. Rose pink and mother of pearl are also sometimes used. The colours visualized should be those found in nature, notably those of flowers like daffodils and bluebells, or of their foliage.

The solar plexus is one of the body's seven major psychic centres or *chakras*, the others being the brow centre, which is located between the eyebrows, the crown centre (at the back of the head), the throat centre, the heart centre, the sacral centre, and the base centre. There are also 21 minor centres and a further 49 small centres, any of which may be used depending upon the ailment being treated.

Treatment begins by clearing the aura of its residues by 'sweeping' it with the hands. Ronald Leech says that the residues are often seen as a grey-coloured mist by sensitives. When that has been done, the colour healer begins to work on one of the major centres or on one of the minor centres closest to the problem area. Leech explains: 'We direct a colour at a centre to obtain a particular result. One has to concentrate hard. If you can visualize, say, spring green, that's good, but it doesn't matter if you can't because if you think "spring green" there is a law of nature that says "energy follows thought" and the energy goes there. If we wanted to enliven or give a tonic to a person, we would apply one of the sunlight colours, gold or possibly even orange, to the spleen. That is not one of the major centres but it is one of the important minor centres. However, it is very seldom that any other colour but sapphire blue is used on the solar plexus, although the other centres can have a range of colours passed through them. Each treatment can take from 40 minutes to one hour, and a number of treatments are required depending on what is wrong with a person.'

Diagnosis at a Distance

Many medical dowsers are able to diagnose at a distance by holding a pendulum over a 'map' of the patient, which is usually a line drawing of the human body or, in the case of sick animals, one of the particular animal type.

The medical dowser Gail Yulden (not her real name), who is based in Lockerbie, Scotland, does most of her dowsing over drawings of the horses, cows, dogs and cats that she specializes in treating. She is assisted in such distance dowsing by placing a witness of the sick animal, which may be a specimen of its hair or a nail clipping, on the drawing. In this way she can pick out the part that is injured or diseased and then, by dowsing over that part, determine exactly what is wrong with the animal. But she still makes house calls, travelling up to 200 miles each day, and although she doesn't visit all the sick animals she is asked to treat, she estimates that she sees about 50 per cent of them.

'I go to look at the situation in which they're kept, the

circumstances in which their illness has taken place,' she explains. 'The client usually tells me some of the symptoms. They'll say, for example, "My horse is lame, but I don't know why." I do many horses — racehorses, event horses, show jumpers, trotters, and so on — and there was one year when I had on my books the winner of the Gold Cup at Cheltenham, which is a very important race, the winner of the Badminton Horse Trials, and the leading show jumper at Wembley.'

Having determined the nature of the illness, Gail Yulden then uses her pendulum to select the appropriate homoeopathic remedy, one that matches all the symptoms. This is delivered to the owner of the sick animal in the form of homoeopathic pills, which are administered orally. But if the illness or injury is particularly bad, she sends through the air to the animal rays of the substance which begin the healing effect while the pills are in the post.

'It sometimes doesn't matter if they wait a day or two for the pills to arrive,' she says, 'but it's often best if I send them rays while they're waiting.'

But clearly the medical dowser who works over a drawing of an animal or of a human, like the map dowser, cannot be responding to radiated energy disharmonies, but must, as with his (or her) selection of the appropriate remedy, be employing psychic faculties. Indeed, their frequent and successful use adds a further mysterious twist to the practice of dowsing, which suggests that it is a far more complex and biologically sophisticated procedure than at first appears.

CHAPTER SIX

BLACK STREAMS

> Just as we must understand it when it is said, That
> Aesculapius prescribed this man horse-exercise, or
> bathing in cold water, or going without shoes; so
> we must understand it when it is said, That the
> nature of the universe prescribed to this man
> disease, or mutilation, or loss, or anything else
> of the kind.

From the *Meditations* of Marcus Aurelius Antoninus

Conventional or allopathic medicine has been remarkably
successful in discovering the cause of most of the serious
diseases that afflict mankind, which has enabled its
practitioners to sharply reduce their incidence among the
population at large by advocating better public hygiene, a
clean water supply, improved sewage disposal facilities, etc, by
devising effective preventative measures like vaccinations, and
by developing specific drugs to cure diseases when they occur.
And although it is fashionable in some circles to decry its

methods as 'unnatural', the fact remains that our debt to allopathic medicine is enormous. Indeed, readers might like to remind themselves that without it, they would probably not be here.

Yet while conventional medicine has brought great benefits, notably in the prevention and cure of infectious diseases, there still remain a large number of conditions and disorders whose origin is mysterious and whose remedy is unknown.

For example, why do so many people suffer from debilitating migraine headaches? Or from rheumatism? Or arthritis? Or insomnia? Or diabetes? Or ME? Or epilepsy? Or cancer? Or chronic heart conditions? And why, for that matter, are so many people anxious, depressed, and irritable? Most of these disorders have been explained as the products of modern life, but this says nothing about their specific cause.

Causes of Cancer

Let us for a moment consider cancer. Its name is Latin, meaning 'crab', and derives from the crab-like patches observed in melanoma or skin cancer. It is actually a malignant tumour resulting from an uncontrolled growth of tissue cells, which may affect the lungs, the liver, the stomach, the rectum, and other organs or parts, often spreading from one region of the body to another. But despite years of research, the cause of cancer is still improperly understood. For while skin cancer, for example, typically affects those who have spent too long in the sun, by no means all sunbathers contract it. And similarly, while lung cancer has been linked to cigarette smoking, only 10 per cent of heavy smokers develop the disease, a rate which compares with the number of non-smokers so affected.

Hence it looks very much as if while prolonged exposure to strong sunlight and heavy smoking increase the risk of cancer, they do not in themselves cause it. This suggests that there may be another factor in the environment which tips the balance for those at risk, and which is, in this sense, the prime cause of the disease. And this factor will also be the initiator of cancer in those who are not at risk.

Illness and Water Veins

This brings us to the dowser Abbé Mermet, mentioned in the previous chapter, who observed that the incidence of sickness is greater among those living over water veins, and who claimed that their radiations were detrimental to health. He wrote:

> One may be exposed to them in a workshop, a factory, an office, as well as in a flat on the tenth floor of a building. (But) it is in a bedroom that their presence is most harmful for, in such a case, the affected individual is not only subjected to the bad effects of such radiations but is also deprived of sound and regenerating sleep. Impaired health results in consequence, and the affected person suffers from various ailments which neither he nor the doctor can account for.[4]

This is why water veins have been called 'black streams'.

Abbé Mermet's claims were largely ignored until the 1930s when French researchers discovered that the air above water veins contains a higher proportion of ions than normal. This immediately suggested that they were emitting more ionizing radiation in the form of gamma rays than were the surrounding rock strata. Gamma rays have an extremely short wavelength and can easily pass through solids, including thick concrete and steel, which means that the floors and ceilings of a house are no barrier to them. So, if a house is built above one or more water veins, or even above a geological discontinuity like a fault, which also discharges more gamma radiation, its occupants will be subjected to larger doses of such telluric radiation that may cause, at one extreme, insomnia or irritability, or at the other, chronic arthritis or even cancer.

And human beings are not the only living things affected by the noxious radiations of black streams. Farmers who have penned livestock for long periods in sheds and barns erected over water veins have found that they become restless and aggressive, grow slowly, either abort their young or devour those that are born, and are prone to disease. The growth of many plants is likewise deleteriously affected. For example, fruit trees planted above water veins not only grow slowly and have a poor yield, but are less resistant to disease and often develop cancerous tumours. Similarly, the ripening of crops like tomatoes, onions, and carrots, is delayed if the plants are growing above a water vein. And wines that are stored above water veins tend to go sour.

Yet, oddly enough, not all living things are adversely affected. Trees like oaks, willows and ashes remain healthy and vigorous when growing above black streams, and beehives so situated produce more honey than those nearby which are not. In this case one man's meat *is* another man's poison!

Dowsing for Water Veins

The malevolent influence of black streams means that you can put your pendulum or dowsing rod to good use by testing your own home for their presence beneath it. It may be that either you or someone in your house is suffering from, for instance, migraine headaches, or insomnia, or is irritable or perhaps depressed. If so, the cause, like that of the other more serious conditions, might be an underground black stream or streams.

It is most important to check out the place where you sleep, for it is while lying in bed, as Abbé Mermet remarked, that we receive the longest exposure to gamma rays emitted by water veins. You should also test the armchair where you habitually sit, as if it lies above a water vein, you will be subjected to above-average levels of gamma-radiation while you take your ease in it. In fact you should check out any spot where you frequently sit or lie.

Some houses and office buildings have the misfortune to be built above water veins that are several feet wide, which may result in a whole room, and those above it, or even the whole building, being turned into a danger zone. But often the water veins are quite narrow, sometimes only a centimetre or two in width, which results in thin strips of radiation crossing the rooms beneath which they lie. Indeed, the odd thing about the radiation given out by water veins is that it rises straight up into the air, producing no lateral spread. And because the rays are only harmful after prolonged exposure to them, they present little or no danger to anyone simply walking through them several times a day.

'Hot Spots'

Yet because water veins can lie at different depths beneath a house, they can cross each other without interference, and where they cross they give rise to a 'hot spot' of concentrated radiation. Studies by dowsers have shown that people afflicted by localized complaints often sleep in beds where several water veins cross beneath the place where that particular part of them is positioned. For example, Figure 18 shows the plan of a bed used by a woman who suffered from painful periods, and the dowsed course of water veins beneath it. As can be seen, three water veins cross under the place where her pelvis normally rested.

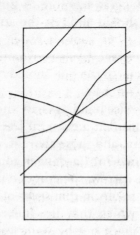

Figure 18: 'Hot spot' caused by three water veins crossing beneath bed of woman suffering from period pains.

Tracing the Course of a Water Vein with a Pendulum

While you can discover the presence and course of underground water veins with any dowsing device, it is easiest to find them indoors using a pendulum.

Most dowsers, myself included, find that the pendulum swings in a circular motion when it is held above a water vein.

Sometimes, however, the pendulum may swing laterally. If so, it makes the general line of the vein. When held above a place where there is no underlying water vein, the pendulum will hang motionless.

When you stand beside, say, your bed you should bear in mind that you want to detect underground water, but it is not necessary to think about this too hard. The best approach, in fact, is simply to form the intention and then forget about it. When you have done that, hold the pendulum above one spot on the bed and watch for any movement. If there is none, go on to test another spot and repeat the procedure until you obtain a dowsing reaction, if any.

If you find that you do get a positive response at one place, mark it with a small piece of paper. Then go on to trace the course of the vein by testing around the spot in the same way. You will eventually find another that gives the same reaction. Mark this like the first. Then, to check that it is the same water vein and not another lying close to it, test the bed on the other side of the first spot. A positive reaction will tell you that it probably is the same vein, which you can confirm by testing farther out. And if each site is identified with a piece of paper, it won't be long before you have marked out the course of the vein. Then go on to search out other veins which may be present, and which perhaps cross the first. You may even locate a point where three or more water veins cross or come close to doing so. At worst, you may even find several such 'hot spots' on the bed.

Re-siting Furniture

Once you have determined that your (or someone else's) bed or favourite armchair is underlain by water veins, you should move it (or them) to a place in the room that isn't. Hence your next task is to survey the rest of the bedroom, or living room, with your pendulum, in order to discover 'cold' areas that have no water veins beneath them. Because the siting of the bed is of critical importance, you may find that if you are unlucky enough to have chosen a room that is criss-crossed with water veins, you may have to move the bed into another room. If you are very unfortunate, you may find your whole house is underlain by one large water vein or so criss-crossed by small water veins that it is unsafe. Such bad luck gives you the uncomfortable option of selling your house and moving elsewhere, although you may feel it is morally wrong to part with it if it is suffused with such potentially dangerous telluric radiation. But it does mean that you should always test each of the downstairs rooms of a potential new home for the presence of underground black streams before agreeing to buy.

Protection Against Gamma Rays

However, there are a couple of ways of protecting yourself against gamma rays. The best, but most expensive, method is to lay a sheet of lead beneath the affected bed or armchair. This will stop the rays in their tracks and render the bed, or whatever, safe. The bad news is that this remedy is not permanent, as the lead sheet will need to be renewed every eight months or so. If the sheet is not changed, the injurious effect of the rays is somehow enhanced, leading to a dramatic worsening of the health condition they may have caused.

Another effective, but far less expensive, method of combating the effects of telluric rays is to paint the floor beneath the bed or armchair blue, or alternatively to lay under them a large sheet of paper which has been painted blue. Blue, a traditionally neutral colour, has the surprising ability to negate water-vein radiation, although how it does this is uncertain. But you can observe its action (and efficiency!) by laying a sheet of blue paper over a 'hot spot' and then testing it again with your pendulum. You should find that you no longer get a dowsing response.

But it is always best, where possible, to reposition frequently-used items of furniture so that they stand over places unaffected by black-stream radiation.

The proof of the pudding is, of course, in the eating. If you suffer from, say, insomnia and have discovered that your bed is standing above one or more water veins, whose emanations may be causing your inability to sleep, then you should sleep better once you have moved it to a safe spot. The same will be true if you get migraine headaches or are unaccountably irritable. But don't expect immediate relief. Indeed, some days may have to pass before an improvement is felt. This is particularly true if you suffer from a more serious condition like arthritis or rheumatism. However, you can rest assured that the complaint will not worsen after the move and that it will, in time, show a definite improvement.

Case Study 1

But in case you're thinking that the link between telluric emissions and human disease is not proven, I would like to mention the work of Gustav Freiherr von Pohl. In 1929 this dowser, watched by local officials, made a survey with his divining rod of the small town of Vilsbiburg, and marked the course of all the large water veins he discovered beneath it on a map of the town. When Vilsbiburg's medical chief plotted the sites of the houses once occupied by people who had died of cancer, it was found that in all cases the house in question was either wholly or partly underlain by one of the veins.

Case Study 2

The benefits of moving a badly-positioned bed were dramatically illustrated in the case of a young girl who was suffering from a double curvature of the spine, which Christopher Bird records in his book *Divining*. In 1975 the American dowser Herbert Douglas plotted the course of several water veins running underneath the girl's bed, and recommended that it be moved to a neutral spot. This was immediately done. For ten days there was an unfortunate increase in the girl's pain, but thereafter her condition remarkably improved, to the extent that her spinal curvature lessened. After several months had gone by, it was found that not only had her pain completely vanished but that she was no longer so deformed that she required a brace.

Even more interesting is the fact that Herbert Douglas has discovered that whenever he tests the beds of people suffering from arthritis, he always finds that they are underlain by water veins.

As a biologist by training, I recognize these discoveries as potentially very important. For if prolonged exposure to black-stream radiation does cause such degenerative illnesses as arthritis and cancer, and if it perhaps predisposes both human beings and animals to infection, then not only could the incidence of disease be sharply reduced by the better siting of homes, offices and factories, but great savings could be made in the cost of health care.

CHAPTER SEVEN

DOWSERS ANCIENT AND MODERN

Quantum phenomena seem to make decisions, to 'know'
what is happening elsewhere. (Indeed) quantum
phenomena may be connected so intimately that
things once dismissed as 'occult' could become
topics of serious consideration among physicists.

From *The Dancing Wu Li Masters* by Gary Zukav.

Dowsing, like any other field of human endeavour, has its stars, those men and women who have excelled at it and who have often raised a storm of controversy by their activities. In this chapter we will look at the lives of some of these people, and meet a present-day professional water diviner, whose methods of working are both interesting and instructive.

Baroness de Beausoleil

Our first dowsing star is a woman — Martine de Bertereau, Baroness de Beausoleil — who during the early years of the seventeenth century travelled extensively in France and in many other European countries locating mineral deposits by dowsing, accompanied by her husband, the Baron de Beausoleil, a mining consultant. In France alone they together discovered over 150 ore deposits of iron, gold and silver, whose whereabouts in the kingdom the Baroness carefully recorded in her book *La Restitution de Pluto*, published in 1640. It was dedicated to the notorious Cardinal Richelieu, the real power behind the French throne, whom the Baroness had hoped to please with her account of the mineral wealth of France. But the Cardinal was far from pleased; in fact he was so scandalized by the authoress's admitted use of the 'black arts', that he promptly had both her and her husband imprisoned in separate fortresses, where they languished, broken-hearted, never to see each other again, until the day that death claimed them.

Jacques Aymar Vernay

On July 25th, 1692, just over fifty years after the publication of *La Restitution de Pluto*, a dreadful crime was committed which brought another dowser widespread renown, but ultimately disgrace and humiliation. For on that day, in the southern French town of Lyons, a wine merchant and his wife were robbed and then brutally murdered with a meat cleaver, much to the outrage and alarm of their fellow citizens, who demanded that the perpetrators be arrested and punished. The town guard, having no obvious clues to go on, in desperation turned to the dowser Jacques Aymar Vernay, a poor mason living in the nearby village of Saint Marcellin, in Dauphiné province, where he had gained a considerable reputation for himself by being able to find, with his dowsing rod, not only the sites of underground sources of water and ore bodies, but also the whereabouts of criminals.

Brought to the scene of the crime, Aymar, as he is usually known, impressed all by first accurately pin-pointing the places where the two bodies had lain. He then led the town guard and a crowd of interested sightseers to one of the city's gates, which gave access to the bridge crossing the river Rhone. This being locked for the night, the party waited until the following day, and then were led by Aymar across the bridge and downstream to a gardener's house, where the dowser stopped, went inside, and found three chairs standing around a table, on which stood an empty bottle of wine. Aymar tested the bottle and each of the three chairs with his rod, and obtaining an affirmative response, announced that the murderers, three in number, had temporarily broken their flight there to drink the wine. The appearance of three ruffianly men at the house the day before was confirmed by the absent gardener's two children, who related how the trio had suddenly turned up, forced their way inside, and emptied the wine bottle before running off along the bank of the river.

Taking up the hunt again, Aymar next led his companions to the town of Beaucaire, where his dowsing rod, oddly enough, directed him to the prison. The warden was persuaded to bring out all his recently arrested criminals, thirteen in number, who were made to line up, while Aymar, standing before each in turn with his rod, found that it dipped before just one of them, a hunchback who had only been incarcerated one hour earlier. This man, announced Aymar, was one of the robbers, although he had not himself taken part in the murders.

The hunchback at first protested his innocence, but when he was later identified as having been seen near the vintner's shop on the day of the murders, he broke down and confessed to having helped his two accomplices, both strangers to the area, to commit the crime. These, he added, had now left the province. The search for them was immediately begun, with Aymar taking the lead with his dowsing rod, and continued all the way to the Mediterranean port of Toulon, where the dowser found the inn at which they had stayed before boarding a boat to the Italian port of Genoa. But unfortunately, because the killers had left the French kingdom, they could not be pursued any farther and the hunt for them was abandoned. The hunchback, however, paid for his part in the robbery by being tried, found guilty, and condemned to death by being broken on the wheel. In fact he was the last person in Europe to be so executed.

Aymar's success in both finding one of the criminals and in identifying the places where he and the others had temporarily taken refuge caused a sensation. He became something of a celebrity, and was to further demonstrate his skill by tracking down criminals in other towns. And when a book, entitled *Occult Physics* and written by Pierre le Lorrain, Abbé de Vallemont, appeared the following year, which mentioned his extraordinary abilities, Aymar was brought to the attention of the Prince de Condé, who persuaded him to come to Paris and take part in some tests.

In one test, the Prince had six holes dug in a garden. He left one hole empty, filled one with gravel, and placed different kinds of metals in the other four. He then had the holes carefully plugged with grass sods. Aymar was brought into the garden and asked to locate the holes containing metal. The dowser strode gallantly about the garden, his rod dipping at only two spots. These, he said, were the sites of the metals. Yet when the sod plugs were lifted, one hole was seen to be empty, while the other was filled with gravel. Thus Jacques Aymar Vernay, in the opinion of those watching, had failed the test completely. And he did little better in the other tests devised by the Prince, which undermined his credibility.

The dowser's reputation was damaged further by the publication of a list of his other mistakes, including an account of how he had tried to identify those women who had been unfaithful to their husbands, an act which had caused much distress to the families concerned. This led to the issuing of an edict against dowsing, which the Church condemned as a Devilish practice. And following it, Jacques Aymar, once the hero of the hour, vanished into obscurity.

Barthelemy Bléton

But despite such attacks, the popularity of dowsing as a method of locating water and precious metals continued to grow in France, although it was used less often for the resolution of moral issues. And it was in France during the eighteenth century that one of the most remarkable dowsers of all time was born. His name was Barthelemy Bléton, and he too, like Jacques Aymar, was a scion of the province of Dauphine. His dowsing talents were a natural gift.

Bléton was unusual in that, in common with a number of modern dowsers, he was very sensitive to the presence of water flowing underground, which made him feel quite ill, so that he did not need to use a dowsing rod to detect it. But when he was prevailed upon to use one by those who wished to test his abilities, he chose not a forked rod, but a straight one, which he held bent into a slight arc. This reacted to the dowsing signal by rotating on its axis at a rate that varied from 30 to 80 times a minute and which seemed thereby to mirror the rate of flow of the water through the vein.

Bléton was first tested by the Bishop of Grenoble, who found him to be incredibly accurate in locating underground water sources. Indeed, it is even said that Bléton, by discovering the whereabouts of many underground springs in one dry region of France, 'converted a desert into a fruitful country'.

His fame brought him to the attention of Dr Pierre Thouvénel, one of the physicians attendant upon King Louis XVI, who began to study the dowser in 1780 and who produced two detailed reports of his findings in 1781 and 1784 respectively. Thouvénel used Bléton's remarkable talents to locate the source of mineral water lying near to the town of Contrexéville, in eastern France, which turned the quiet country seat into a busy medicinal resort that is still in business today. He also, during the course of his experiments, claimed to show that the movements of Bléton's rod were caused by the electrical field generated by subterranean flowing water. His conclusions in this regard are similar to those of the Quebec geophysicist Professor Michel Chouteau, of whom more later.

Following Thouvénel's first report a commission was set up to examine Bléton's talents more closely. In one experiment Bléton was asked to trace the course of an underground aqueduct, which he followed without error, despite the hidden tunnel's numerous twists and turns, several miles out into the country. And even more incredibly, Bléton subsequently repeated this feat, blindfolded, in front of an incredulous crowd of scientists, government ministers and foreign diplomats.

But despite these successes there were many in the scientific establishment who refused to believe in either Thouvénel's 'electrical effluvia' or in Bléton's supposed ability to detect them. The doctor's experiments were criticized as being unscientific, while Bléton was subjected to further tests supervised by those who believed him to be a fraud. And hardly surprisingly, the sensitive Bléton, much to the satisfaction of his opponents, failed to produce positive results.

Such hostility caused both Thouvénel and Bléton to flee

France for the kinder shores of Italy. Yet the strain of exile was to prove too much for Bléton, who died shortly thereafter, another victim of 'scientific' closed-mindedness.

John Mullins

The following century saw the emergence of a number of excellent dowsers, of whom none was more remarkable than the Englishman John Mullins. A Wiltshire farmer by profession, Mullins practised dowsing in his spare time and became so good at finding underground water sources that his fame spread far beyond the borders of his native county. This resulted in him being asked on several occasions to dowse for water in areas where he had never been before and about which he knew nothing.

One example of his skill shows how, if he had been consulted at the outset, he would have saved the company concerned a good deal of time and money.

In 1887 the bacon factory of Richardson & Co., at Waterford, southern Ireland, had need of much more water to cope with the expansion of its business. The owners therefore asked some geological consultants to advise them where they should sink a bore-hole. And acting on the advice received they sunk a 292 ft (86.7m) bore-hole through a bed of extremely hard rock, only to find nothing more than a totally inadequate trickle of water.

The next year, after taking further geological advice, another bore-hole was sunk, this time at the bottom of a 62 ft (18.6 m) well, first to a depth of 612 ft (183.6 m) and then, having failed to 'strike' water, another 338 ft (101.4 m). But the result was the same: no water was located. Further consultations with geologists took place, who recommended a third site, but when the drilling revealed the same underlying strata as had been previously encountered, the geologists concluded that there was no water on land adjoining the bacon factory and told the owners that they would have to move the factory to another place.

Now desperate, the owners decided to call in the services of John Mullins, who was brought across to Waterford from Wiltshire early in 1889. The dowser was told nothing about the efforts that had already been made to find water and was simply given the run of the property. Mullins set to work walking about with his dowsing rod, until at one spot it turned down with such force that it broke in his hands. He informed the owners that if they sunk a bore-hole there they would tap an abundant supply of water between 80 and 90 ft (24-27 m) down. He then proceeded to locate two other sites which, he said, would prove equally fruitful.

Boring was immediately started at the first site, and a depth of 88 ft (26.4 m), just as Mullins had predicted, a copious supply of good, fresh water gushed out, which was to give a steady flow of between 3,000 and 5,000 gallons (13,620-22,700 litres) per hour, quite sufficient to satisfy the demands of the bacon factory. The geologists, while embarrassed by their failure, said that the dowser must have discovered a fissure in the underlying rock through which water was flowing from nearby hills, although there was no sign of this at the surface, the water-containing rock being covered by a 40 ft (12 m) thick bed of boulder clay.

The bacon factory's owners were delighted with the result, and naturally wished that they had brought in Mullins sooner.

Mullins was tested in some experiments carried out by the Hon. Murray Finch-Hatton, M.P. for South Lincs (1884–5), whose distant ancestor, the third Earl of Winchelsea, distinguished himself by fathering 27 children. One of the experiments rather nicely showed that dowsers are sensitive to the presence of underground water that is flowing, but fail to respond to water that is stagnant. Finch-Hatton wrote:

> On reaching the kitchen garden I knew that a lead pipe, leading water to a tap outside the wall, crossed the gravel path at a certain spot. On crossing it the twig made no sign. I was astonished at first, until I remembered what Mullins had said about stagnant water and that the tap was not running. I sent to have it turned on, re-conducted Mullins over the ground, when the twig immediately indicated the spot. When Mullins had passed on I carefully marked the exact spot indicated by the twig. When he had left the garden, I said: 'Now, Mullins, may we blindfold you and let you try?' He said, 'Oh yes, if you don't lead me into a pond or anything of that sort.' We promised. I then re-conducted him blindfolded to the marked spot by a different route, leaving the tap running, with the result that the stick indicated with mathematical exactness the same spot. At first he slightly overran a foot or so and then felt round, as it were, and seemed to be led back to the exact centre of influence by the twig.[5]

Michael Cranfield

Michael Cranfield, who resides at East Burnside, Clackmannanshire, is one of Britain's few full-time dowsers, although he prefers to be known as a 'water-diviner'. A gaunt, craggy man, whose face looks as if it has been cut from the granite rocks of Scotland over which he tirelessly tramps, he has been dowsing for more than fifty years, yet only became a professional when he retired from an otherwise busy life as a farm milk-bar owner. He works with the traditional Y-shaped hazel rod, which turns upwards for him when he finds water.

Indeed, he only looks for water. He has, he admits, been singularly unsuccessful at finding other things.

He was introduced to dowsing as a teenager, by a friend of his parents, a Naval officer named Clive Lowe, recently returned from Ceylon, who demonstrated how he used a dowsing rod to determine why the new runway at Trincomalee was sagging.

'My brother and I had a go with it on my father's lawn,' he recalls, 'and I found that I could do it quite easily. And then of course having acquired that knowledge I tucked it away and used it as and when required.'

As well as being one of only two full-time dowsers that he knows of in Scotland, Michael Cranfield is unique in being part of a dowsing team. His associate is Morag Syne, a jolly woman who specializes in doing the preparatory map work before he takes to the field with his dowsing rod. About 60 per cent of their clients are farmers, and they are typically asked to provide supplementary water for stock and for domestic use, or occasionally to make a pond.

'You see, times have changed,' he explains. 'The ecology has changed. Farming isn't profitable, so therefore the farmer is carrying more beasts to keep his profit margin. Therefore he wants more water. A certain amount may be supplied by the Water Authority, and we look for the rest.'

Together he and Morag have so far dowsed between 80 and 90 usable water veins, with an accuracy approaching 100 per cent. In fact he remembers only one failure, which came about because the driller went to the wrong place. But as the driller later found water, nobody complained.

Their system of operation is simple and straightforward.

'I first ask the client to produce a map and tell me where he would like us to try and find water. He'll say, "I'd like it here, or here," and so on. We then dowse the map with a pendulum, which we work over it very slowly, starting from the places where the water is desired, and then fanning out from them if necessary. It's a bit laborious perhaps, but it's accurate. We then go out and I am steered to the point(s) on the ground that we have marked on the map. I get a feeling in my body before the rod starts to move.'

Indeed, Michael's bodily sensations are of paramount importance, as he walks over the potential site, holding his dowsing rod, with his eyes shut. This means of course that the movement of the rod is not prompted by visual signals subconsciously received. How then does he think dowsing works? He says: 'I can't explain map dowsing, but I can explain outside dowsing. The earth, you know, has a magnetic core, which runs from the south pole to the north pole, and it sends out waves of magnetism which when they strike water change in composition, and that enables us dowsers to pick up that on our rod and transfer it to our muscles, which contract and move it.'

Drilling invariably follows dowsing because most water veins large enough to supply a steady flow of water lie too deep to be dug down to. And in Scotland, Michael Cranfield observes, once drilling has been completed and a casing inserted into the bore-hole, the water has to be pumped to the surface.

'A modern dowser has got to be a good businessman,' he notes. 'He's got to have very good communication with his client and his driller. And of course he must be able to write reports.'

He hopes to continue dowsing for many years, despite his somewhat frail health. He loves to feel the wind in his hair and the soft squash of heather beneath his feet. And the joy of finding water is a constant delight. He is quick, however, to include Morag in all his many successes.

'We're a team,' he sighs. 'It's a lovely thing to have your team mate along with you. I don't think there has been a team of dowsers before. We're pretty special in that way!'

AFTERWORD

A funeral stone,
Or verse, I covet none;
But only crave
Of you, that I may have
A sacred laurel springing from my grave.

From *To Laurels* by Robert Herrick.

The most recent piece of research into dowsing that I came across while writing this book took place in the summer of 1989. It involved the French-Canadian dowser Michel Petit, a resident of Sherbrooke, Quebec, and a psychologist by profession, who wanted to know what signal he was responding to when he successfully located, as he often did, water and minerals. He contacted Radio-Canada, the French section of the Canadian Broadcasting Corporation, and a producer there arranged for an experiment to be carried out with him by Professor Michel Chouteau, a geophysicist at the Ecole Polytechnic in Montreal.

Petit uses a dowsing rod made from strips of whalebone, three of which are bound together to form each of its two arms, these being united at one end to produce the flexible Y-shaped rod. When held by him, Petit's dowsing rod is unusual in that it turns upwards and towards him when the dowsing signal is received, and then rolls completely over. In fact it may turn over several times when he is walking across an underground water source or an ore body.

The dowser was flown to a remote mining area near Val d'Or in north-western Quebec, which was quite unknown to him but which had been thoroughly investigated by Professor Chouteau. There he was asked to locate, with his dowsing rod, economic deposits of sulphite minerals, such as iron sulphite and copper sulphite. He was accompanied by Professor Chouteau and a television crew who recorded what was done and the outcome. Professor Chouteau told me: 'What we did first was to drive him through one area blindfolded with his dowsing rod, and whenever he got a signal we would mark the site with a little flag. Then he went on foot without a blindfold to survey the area more precisely. We then compared his reactions with the maps we had, and we found that his reactions were really quite accurate. Indeed, I would estimate that he was able to find the mineral veins I knew about with an 80 per cent accuracy.'

Two larger-scale experiments were next carried out. The first required Michel Petit to dowse for minerals while being slowly driven blindfolded a distance of $62^1/2$ miles (100 km) and back again, the second involved the same procedure over a distance of $12^1/2$ miles (20 km) in a different area. The blindfold worn in all the tests ensured that Petit could not respond to any visual clues which might have helped him. And to prevent him possibly receiving any telepathic information from Professor Chouteau, the scientist did not accompany him on any of his journeys. Professor Chouteau describes what happened: 'But unfortunately, the correlation with what we knew of the second areas was not all that good. On the long trip there was only about a 20 per cent correlation, and on the other there was about a 50 per cent correlation. To explain that Petit said that he'd never dowsed for so long at a time before. And it was tiring for him. His hands were sweating and his arms were aching.'

By measuring the various physical signals to which Michel Petit might have been responding, Professor Chouteau was able to eliminate gravitational changes and varying magnetic fields as being the cause of the rod's movements. He did, however, find a strong correlation between them and the electrical conductivity of the mineral deposits.

'The main conclusion is that if there's anything that is detectable by physical means in finding water and minerals, it is electrical conductivity. For example, the water flowing through the ground, through cracks, produces a voltage charge. Hence it could be that dowsers are sensitive to electrical fields.'

But despite this tentative conclusion, Professor Chouteau appreciates that even if electrical fields do cause the dowser's arm and hand muscles to contract and thus move the rod he is holding, they cannot explain map dowsing or other distance dowsing. He concedes: 'There is no physical phenomenon involved in map dowsing. It could be mental, the manifestation of thoughts, something like that. If it's mental it's very difficult to carry out experiments that are repeatable and that can be done in the lab or in the field. In fact there are many phenomena that we are not aware of that could be involved. This is only the beginning.'

But while the scientists are still struggling to explain dowsing, don't let their knitted brows and inconclusive results stop you from trying, for dowsing, as I have said before, works, whether it can be explained or not. And that in itself should encourage you to have a go yourself, for by doing so you will participate in something that is essentially mysterious, something that seems to operate at the narrow border between matter and spirit, where the ancient gods and dryads join hands with the world of man, and thereby direct your dowsing rod to the treasures lying within Hades' dark and hidden realm.

REFERENCES

Chapter One
1 Homer's *Odyssey*, translated by George Chapman; Book X, lines 322–326.
2 Virgil's *Aeneid*, translated by W.F. Jackson Knight; Book VI.

Chapter Three
3 Plutarch's *Lives*, translated by John and William Langhorne; Volume II, pp. 167–168.

Chapter Six
4 Christopher Bird, *Divining*, Macdonald and Jane's.

Chapter Seven
5 *Encyclopaedia of Psychic Science*, Dowsing, Citadel Press (1974), p. 99.

BIBLIOGRAPHY

Adventure Unlimited by Evelyn Penrose.

Are You Sleeping in a Safe Place? by Rolf Gordon. Dulwich Health Society, 130 Gypsy Hill, London, SE19 1RL.

Divining — the art of searching for water, oil, minerals and other natural resources or anything lost, missing or badly needed by Christopher Bird. Macdonald and Jane's.

Dowsing for you by Bruce Copen. Academic Publications, Dane Hill, Sussex, RH17 7EX.

Dowsing: Techniques and Applications by Tom Graves. Turnstone Books.

Earth Radiation by Kathe Bachler. Wordmaster, Parkfield House, Parkfield Road South, Didsbury, Manchester, M20 0DB (1988).

Harmful Radiations and their Elimination by Bruce Copen. Academic Publications.

Water Witching U.S.A. by Evon Z. Vogt and Ray Hyman. The University of Chicago Press (1979).

SOME USEFUL ADDRESSES

American Society of Dowsers Inc.
Danville
Vermont 05828-0024
USA

Association of Scottish Dowsers
Riccarton Mill
Newcastleton
Roxburghshire TD9 05Q
Scotland

British Society of Dowsers
Sycamore Cottage
Tamley Lane
Hastingleigh
Ashford
Kent TN25 5HW
England

INDEX